Discussing – Mastering the Skills of Moderation

Leading Discussions, Conducting Surveys, Steering Roundtables and Using Manipulation

Horst Hanisch

Idea and text: Horst Hanisch, Bonn

English editing and translation: Thomas Schommers, Neuss

Layout: Guido Lokietek, Aachen; Horst Hanisch, Bonn

Cover: Christian Spatz, engine-productions, Cologne; Horst Hanisch, Bonn

Pictures: Horst Hanisch, Bonn

Publisher: BoD · Books on Demand GmbH, In de Tarpen 42, 22848 Norderstedt,

bod@bod.de

Printed: Libri Plureos GmbH, Friedensallee 273, 22763 Hamburg

ISBN: 978-3-7693-1596-7

Discussing – Mastering the Skills of Moderation

Leading Discussions, Conducting Surveys, Steering Roundtables and Using Manipulation

Fore-word

"I welcome you ..."

"Don't be afraid of perfection.
You will never reach it."
Salvador Dali, Spanish painter
(1904 - 1989)

"... to our discussion roundtable today."

We talk with each other and we talk to each other. We speak, discuss, carry on, and communicate, etc. Do we listen to each other as well?

"Of course," we may say.

"I am also listening to the other person. Otherwise I wouldn't know how to respond to him."

It seems like listening is an elementary part of communication. In a broader sense we tacitly expect that communication eventually is a goal.

This book considers discussion situations and different kinds of dialogue. Generally, it is assumed that people get together in order to exchange their views.

They also want to present their own opinion – and – in a positive sense, to listen what others have to say.

It is some people's goal to impart as much of their own opinions as possible in a conversation and they are not considerate of other opinions or ideas.

The people who have the largest contribution to a conversation can't necessarily say that their own ideas are the best ones.

It is possible that a quieter person who does want not strongly articulate his opinion actually has brilliant views and contributes greatly to a conversation.

In order to temper the vocal participants and support the passive ones, very often a moderator is used. This person has a few very important duties and responsibilities in a serious discussion.

In the following pages we will look into these details, primarily using one moderator.

This person is attuned to not only the spoken words but also everything else around the discussion. Albert Mehrabian's research indicated that only 7 % of information is transmitted by spoken words.

The other 93 % is transmitted based on how the words are spoken as well as the body language. Experienced moderators consider this knowledge.

They will set the room conditions to achieve the objective of the discussion and use an arrangement that shows respect for each person, relative to their social standing.

While the book by this author "Body Language – in Europe", focuses on nonverbal communication, and the book "Rhetoric – Mastering the Art of Persuasion", primarily focuses on the spoken word, and this book focuses on how to communicate in a group discussion.

The subject is primarily interpersonal in nature, and therefore, we apologize to the reader if we go in more detail in certain areas and if it gives the impression that something might seem to be subjective.

In order to be as objective as possible I have – in my freedom as the author and as a human being - access to other people's experience and knowledge.

Therefore I will use this opportunity to say "THANK YOU!" to everybody who supported me physically and psychological in this project.

There are my students who gave me inspirations through the realization of different group discussions, as well as my father Alfred Hanisch, who supported me as lector and mentor, and my friend Thomas Sturm, who let me work on this project without having too much stress by taking care of all the daily work and duties.

I also do not forget all the other people and friends who gave me small but important and precious suggestions and help.

I wish you, dear reader, lots of fun reading this book and hopefully it is a help for practical implementation, so you can use it for a more successful private and business life!

Horst Hanisch

8

Table Of Contents

Chapter 1 – Reciprocal Interdependency and Influence

What A says and B understands

"When I judge my brother,
I can be mistaken,
if I forgive him, then not."
Karl Heinrich Waggerl, Austrian writer
(1897 - 1973)

Constantly reciprocal influence

In a dialogue or a conversation all participates influence each other.

They also influence the moderator, and the moderator always influences the participants.

Therefore it makes sense to obtain information about the participants of a discussion group beforehand.

This is especially important if you have the responsibility to control and lead the conversation round, i.e., you are the moderator.

Tone of the moderator

The tone of the moderator towards the participants significantly influences the development of a discussion.

If the tone seems to be presumptuous, arrogant, anxious, obedient, etc, the participants will react towards this type of behavior. The correct tone is to be 'self-confident' and 'equal' towards all participants.

It does not matter if the participant is unemployed or a university professor – for the moderator everybody should have an 'equal value'.

Who are the listeners?

Think about, or ask your client in advance, which target group can be expected. For example:

- Pupils
- Trainees
- Vocational pupils
- Students
- Homemakers
- Employees
- Supervisors
- Managers
- Self-employed
- Pensioners
- Unemployed
- Women
- Men
- Foreigners
- Physically disabled
- Self-payers (seminar fee)
- Invitees
- Family
- Friends
- Tradesmen/women
- Academics
- Nobles
- Socially disadvantaged persons
- People with a strong social background
- and others

A speech can be fine-tuned to address each target group in a slightly different way, for example by paying close attention to choice of words or approach – while bearing in mind our statement above that every group is of equal value.

Interdependency among each other

'As the question, so the answer!'

But what is meant by that?

Some moderators make the mistake of dealing with their participants 'just' as a serial number, i.e., as an exchangeable item.

Therein lies a great risk.

The participant may be sensitive. He feels exactly how somebody is dealing with him. He will act towards the moderator the same way.

If the moderator sees the participant 'just as a trainee', then participant will see the moderator 'just as a smart aleck'.

That does not appear to be a solid foundation for a good co-operation. Therefore an appeal to all moderators and conversation-leaders:

"See your participants as interesting individuals who invest their energy to spend a short part of their life with you in order to take home some new knowledge at the end of the conversation."

The audience's needs

Every person has needs – including your counterparties in conversations. According to the U.S. psychologist Abraham Harold Maslow (1908-1970), human beings have the following needs (simplified description):

Human beings have motives and needs. Through fulfillment of their needs, humans become motivated. According to Maslow, motivation has a hierarchical character.

Only when the fundamental needs are fulfilled, can one of the next higher needs come into focus.

The needs are ordered in 5 levels, one on top of the other. Each lower level need has to be fulfilled before the next, higher-level need, can be addressed.

1st Level:

physical needs / physiological needs

This include: food, drink, sleep, motion, self-preservation, sexuality, warmth.

2nd Level:

security needs

This include: physical security, security of minimum sustenance, general protection, retirement arrangements, insurance, need to live in stability, love or sympathy in terms of feeling secure.

3rd Level:

love needs, social needs

This include: affiliation to a social group or society, circle of friends, acquaintanceships, love or sympathy in terms of attention, social clubs or associations.

4th Level:

appreciation needs, self-orientation needs

This include: needs for one's self, recognition though other people, status, power, respect from other people, self-respect, self-confidence, craving for recognition.

5th Level:

need for self-actualization

This include: needs for one's inner self, room for self-fulfillment, room for self-actualization, privacy, realization of one's own possibilities.

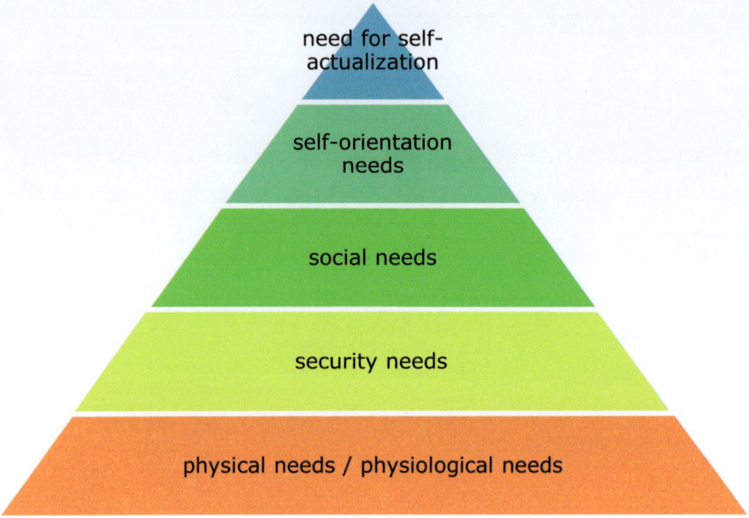

Here, you possibly find the so-called "flow-effect": the ability to capture and achieve a state of happiness (according to happyologist Mihaly Csikszentmihalyi, 1934-2021, [pronounced: Tschik-zent-mihai]).

Examples for consideration of the needs:

Somebody listening becomes tired and therefore he has the need to get some sleep. Maybe he is also hungry and because of that he needs to eat.

In both cases it will be difficult for the participant to concentrate on the presentation. The needs of the listener are more important than his desire to listen and therefore he will become inattentive. He may even begin to disturb the speaker.

Therefore the speaker should always have the needs of his audience in mind and give the participants sufficiently timed opportunities to satisfy their needs. Here are some concrete examples: adequate planning for breaks, layout/environment of the seminar room (air, light, seating arrangements, etc.), organizational (where are the restrooms, where can people smoke, what are the rules of participation?)

Crowds = large audiences

In case you have to speak in front of a large audience, here are some considerations to maintain their attention:

Mass-communication

People who know how to influence the masses have significant power. They have the power to manipulate in a positive as well as in a negative sense.

Of course, the audience knows as well how to resist this kind of manipulation.

Masses and the media

The term 'mass-media' is well known but not clearly defined. It can include:

- newspapers,
- magazines,
- social media,
- broadcast,
- television,
- internet
- sound recording medium,
- and others.

In terms of masses, we differentiate between medial mass and present mass.

Medial mass include, for example, the television audience; those who watch a TV program are <u>unconnected</u> to each other.

Present mass groups are connected to each other and include, for example, the audience attending an open-air-concert. They coexist <u>together</u>.

Therefore, the media builds a bridge between the place of the event and its particular audience.

Influencing a crowd

In order to influence a crowd of people and to capture their interest, the following points can be used:

- activate their basic emotions
  - sympathy, grief
- choose what to address (subject matter)
  - what the majority of the group thinks is right (generally believe or opinion), it is easy to strengthen this

- chose a "fellow human" being approach
    - well-known figure, celebrity
- moral bonus
    - the value of moral points is very high

Crowd behavior

What is the difference in the behavior of a person in his everyday life compared to his behavior in a crowd?

In a crowd, the rationality-control of a single person is interfered by the collective instinct-control of a crowd.

Therefore, an individual will behave, for example, even in an emergency situation or under psychological pressure, in conformity with the group.

That point makes it relatively easy for mass-media to propagate their own opinion on potentially fruitful ground.

Catch the interest of potential participants

What good is a really interesting topic if no one knows it's going to be addressed? What good is a persuasive presentation if nobody is there to listen?

This is why a topic has to be packaged in a way that arouses the curiosity of potential listeners. For example:

- Single Parenthood plus a Full-Time Job – How Do You Manage?
- Do You Know Your Rights? – Labour Law for Workers
- Living with Adolescents – Crisis or Opportunity?
- Making a Good First Impression – The First 7 Seconds Count
- The Winner – Strategies for Greater Self-Confidence
- Children Need Limits – But Which Ones?

Titles with a question mark?

Which title will probably spark more interest and sounds more authoritative?

- 'Women Are More Intelligent' or 'Are Women More Intelligent?'
- 'Eating Bananas Makes You Slim' or 'Does Eating Bananas Make You Slim?'

If the title is already a statement, the presenter has already determined the outcome. This means that, even before the lecture or presentation begins, the listener is faced with a foregone conclusion. This takes all the suspense out of the event.

But if the title is instead presented as a question – simply thrown out without yet being proven, then the participants don't know yet what the answer will be.

- Will We Ever Achieve Immortality?

This kind of title is sure to provoke curiosity and/or suspense. The participant's interest is piqued and he might ask himself:

- "Hm, let's see what the latest scientific findings are."
- "I'd really like to know how that could be."
- "I can't imagine. Could it really be possible?"

Titles with exclamation points!

- 'School Makes You Stupid!' or 'Americans Are Too Fat!'

This kind of title is another way of calling attention – provocatively – to the topic. Beware, though, because titles with exclamation points often prompt:

- burgeoning aggression
  - For example in teachers: "They must be crazy to make such a claim."
  - For example in fat people: "I'm not going to go there just to be embarrassed."

or

- malicious glee
  - For example in opponents of the school system: "That's just what I always say."
  - For example in thin people: "Well, they're certainly not talking about me."

If the goal of the presentation is to encourage a subsequent discussion with strongly diverging opinions, then a title with an exclamation point might be appropriate.

The title must fit the content

Participants will get impatient if they realize that the expectations they had of the talk based on the title are not met.

A seminar titled

- 10 Tips for Happiness
    - turns out to be only a promotional show for CDs or books.

A seminar titled

- 10 Up-to-the Minute Tax Tips
    - presents tips that have been around forever and that are not even applicable anymore

A seminar titled

- A Trip through Thailand
    - spends 75% of the time describing the lives of Buddhist monks.

People don't have anything against a sensationalist title per se. But any expectations raised must be fulfilled. A product in deceptive packaging can only be sold once.

Same topic – different title

Sometimes a topic is difficult to market. Few people show interest.

Is this because of the price of the seminar, the venue where the presentation is being held, or the time? Or would a spruced-up title help to achieve the desired response?

- 'Equal Rights for Men and Women' or perhaps better 'Women Strike Back: Equal Rights for Men and Women?'
- 'Doing Business on the Internet' or 'Doing Business on the Inter.net!' or even better 'Business@Inter.net!'

In other words: The target group can already be influenced by the choice of title.

- Fit for the Future
- Finding Balance As You Get Older
- Wellness for the Woman Over 50

Meaningless titles

Unlike with films or music, meaningless titles for seminars and lectures might grab attention, but the lack of a description of the content will hardly inspire people to spend their money.

- 'R'
- 'The Hole'
- '23^2'

So it's better to stay away from them!

Which goal is the speaker pursuing?

As a rule, a speaker is trying to 'sell' something to his listeners. By this we mean:

- Selling a product
  - for example a vacuum cleaner.
- Selling a service
  - for example writing a speech.
- Selling an idea
  - for example, to his boss
- Selling his own capabilities
  - for example in a job interview

Most talks are aimed at persuading others. Before your presentation, think about why you want to speak to your listeners in the first place.

Set the goal for your talk in advance.

How to arrange the content of a speech

What is the best way to arrange the content of a speech?

Here are some tips you should keep in mind:

- Stick to the facts and make sure you have them right.
- Choose clear language and convey a clear structure.
- Express your thoughts vividly, i.e. using illustrations.
- Build suspense.
- Suspense curve; pay attention to micro- and macro-planning.
- Repeat the basic idea now and again to remind listeners why they are attending your talk.
- Include some surprises.
- Bring some variety into your presentation.
    - Listeners have a maximum attention span of 20 minutes for the same topic.
- Limit your time. 15 minutes of exciting content are more effective than 30 minutes of boredom.
- Humour is allowed.
- You can incorporate some jokes and use sarcasm.
    - But make sure not to hurt anyone's feelings or to violate any taboos.
- Make sure you tell the truth and keep to the facts.
- Perhaps build on a moral theme or a call to action.
- Present in a goal-oriented fashion.
- Be authentic.
    - Be true to yourself, honest and genuine.

Chapter 2 – Interpersonal Communication

The truth is what the audience understands

"Everybody believes they know the truth and everybody knows a different truth."
Gotthold Ephraim Lessing, German writer (1729 - 1781)

The truth is what B understands and not what A says

The truth is what the listener understands and not what the speaker is saying!

Building on the knowledge we already have, this statement should have our immediate buy-in. Unfortunately, interpersonal communication still leads to a lot of misunderstanding.

Through the sender-receiver-model of Friedmann Schulz von Thun, we will describe the basic the communication-process.

One sender forwards information to a receiver. This information can be verbal or non-verbal.

The sender is the speaker and the receiver is the listener. (If a listener asks a question, he will be the sender and the speaker will be the receiver.)

Look at it from the side of the receiver

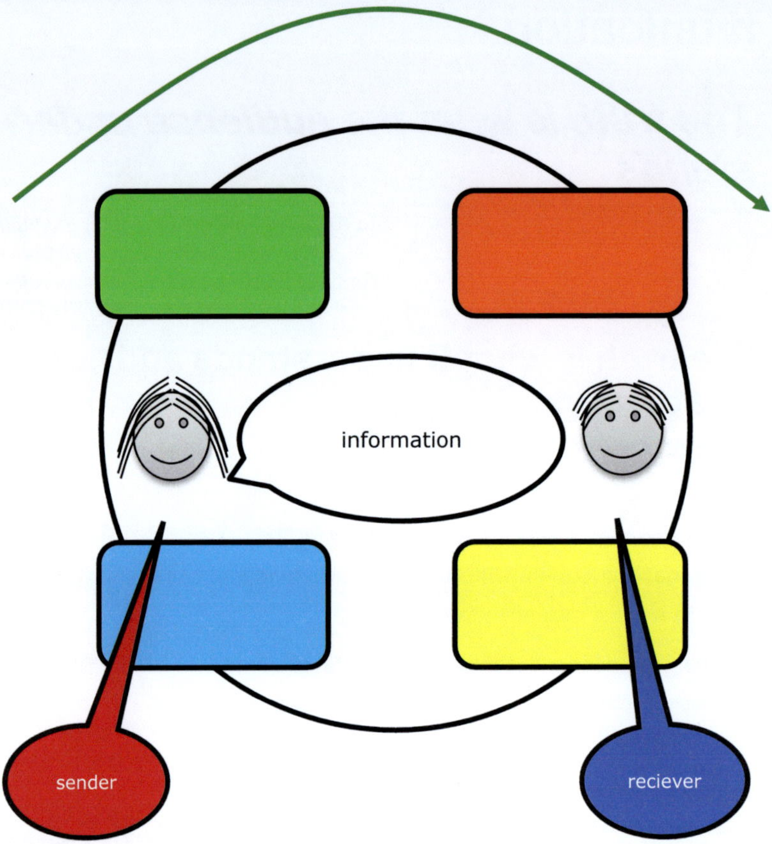

We talk here about false communication: Information is forwarded from a sender to a receiver. S ➔ R.

You will find false communication in television, broadcasting, motion-picture theatre, telefax, printed materials such as newspapers, posters, and also in pictograms, traffic signs, and information signs.

Examples of some pictograms:

- pictogram (pictography):
    - objects are visualized (e.g., illustration [person] for restroom or lavatory)
- ideogram (picture writing):
    - abstract and conventional meaning without recognizable correspondence to reality (e.g., diagonal bar for stopping entry)
- logogram is a word-symbol:
    - symbol, e.g., scientific, mathematic, or logical field
        - + - . :
        - > <
        - [male, female]
        - @

In the following section we will primarily focus on verbal communication in a dialogue of between two people.

According to Schulz von Thun, a message can be delivered through four windows.

- window of content
- window of appeal
- window of relationship
- window of self-revelation

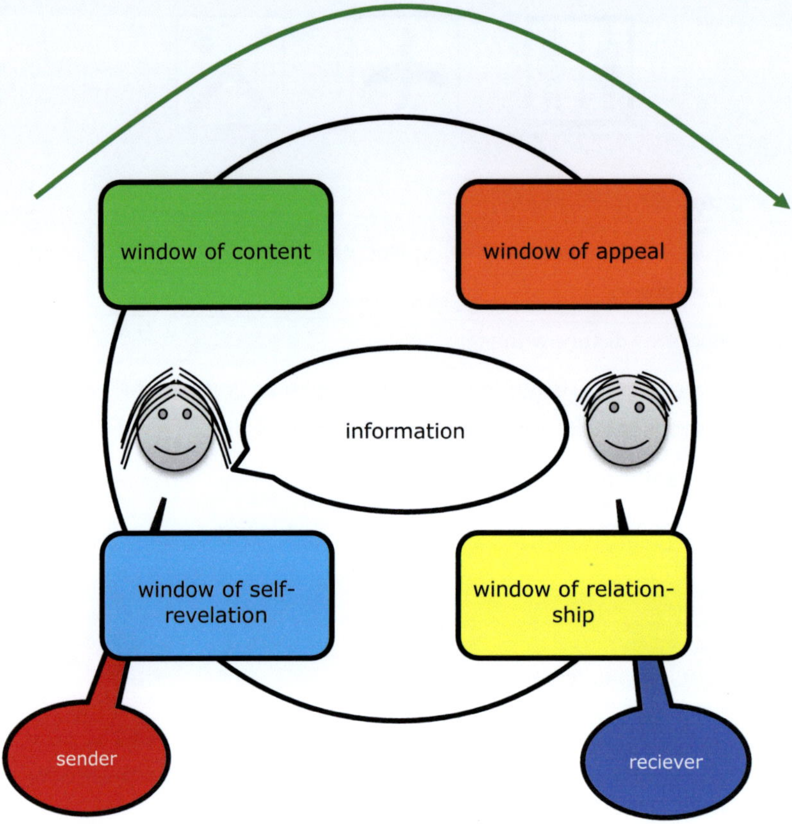
window of content
window of appeal
information
window of self-revelation
window of relation-ship
sender
reciever

The sender can ask himself the following questions for the four windows:

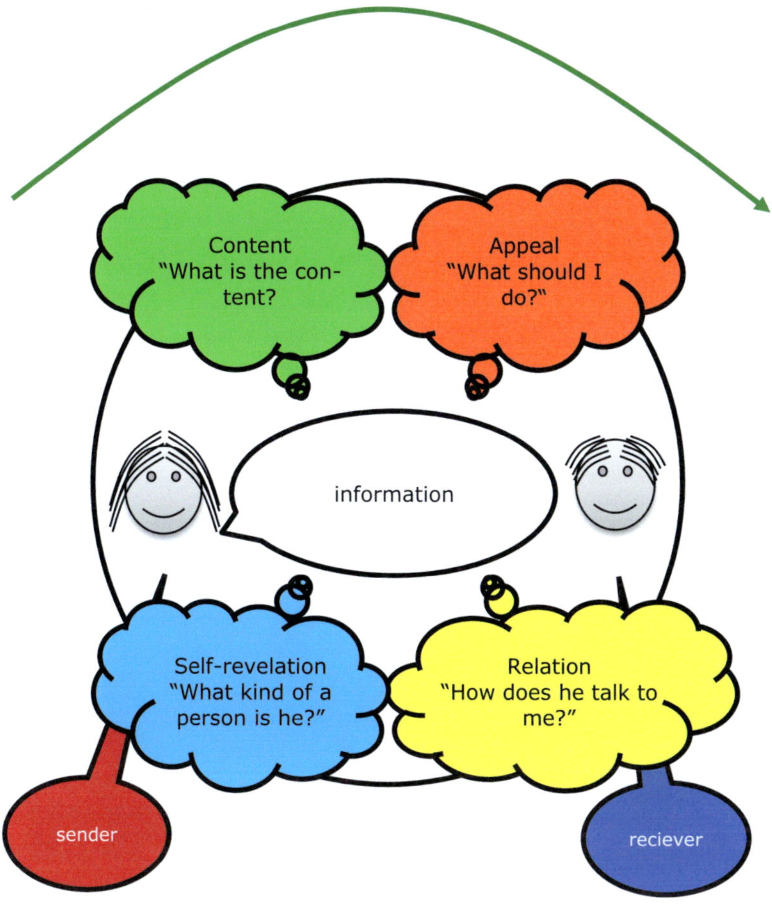

- Window of content: What is the content?
- Window of appeal: What should I do, think, feel?
- Window of relationship: How is the sender talking to me? Who does he think he is talking to?
- Window of self-revelation: What kind of a person is the sender? What is the matter with him?

All people have to die

Example: Information / statement of a speaker: "All people have to die."

Possible interpretation with the help of the four windows

Window of content

- receiver hears the following content:
    - In fact, all people have to die. Just information.

Window of appeal

- receiver hears the following appeal:
    - "Enjoy your life because all people have to die!" or:
    - „I should be cautious", etc.

Window of relationship

- receiver hears the following relationship:
    - "Does he think I'm stupid and don't know that?" or:
    - "Does he want to console me (e.g., in case of funeral)?"

Window of self-revelation

- receiver hears the following self-revelation:
    - "He is totally depressed!" or:
    - "He enjoys his life every day – he is not afraid of death (anymore)."

The receiver can hear four different interpretations from the information "all people have to die". Unfortunately, the receiver does not know which of the four windows the speaker wanted to address.

Did he just want to open the window of content, i.e., forward information or did he want to give an appeal, or …?

Let's assume he wanted to forward with his window content but the receiver opens his relationship window.

In this case they do not understand each other. Professor Paul Anton Watzlawick (1921-2007) calls it punctuation. Both people believe that they are right.

We have the statement that it is true what the listener understands and not what the speaker says. Therefore it is clearly the responsibility of the speaker to clarify which window he wants to open.

In order to figure out if the receiver understood the right meaning it is helpful to ask for confirmation (e.g., feedback).

This way the speaker can realize if the listener's thinking is 'synchronized'.

This approach is achieved through the above-mentioned interaction.

Through the exchange real communication will take place:

S ➔ R and R ➔ S.

Through reciprocal exchange, a communication-cycle develops.

Then, our diagram appears as follows:

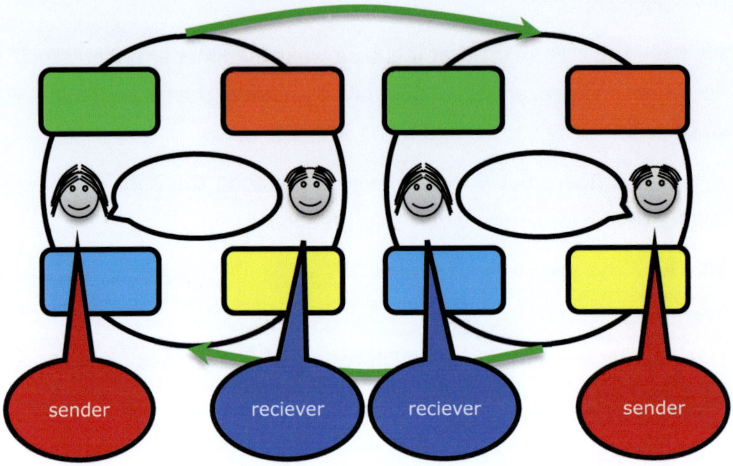

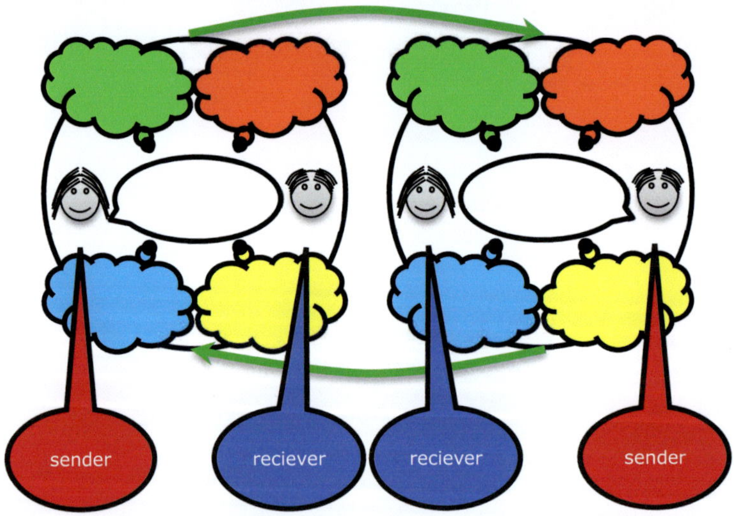

As the exchange is occurring, the speaker could be trying to use any of the four windows.

If you imagine this, it is seems to be a miracle that two people are able to understand each other properly.

Self-influence

The receiver has his own so-called self-concept which he uses (unconsciously) to influence the received information.

He influences the received information and himself through

- the picture the receiver has of the sender,
- listening to a second message, and
- through the effect of the 'self-fulfilling-prophecy': I understand what I want to understand.

Information is characterized though:

- the context (in connection with the information)
- form of verbalization
- corresponding body movements (facial expression/gestures)
- tone of voice

Communication takes place on an objective and emotional layer and therefore it is essential for the participants to actively listen to each other.

Active listening means: the speaker empathizes with the world of the sender and through his own eyes (empathy: psychological capability to put oneself into somebody else's place).

When the speaker and the listener agree with each other how to communicate together (e.g., request to speak desirable but interjections not welcome), this is called meta-communication.

Meta-communication means here: communication about communication, i.e., sender and receiver talk about their communication.

Chapter 3 – Group Dynamics

Behavior of participants in a conversation

"It is not an act of courtesy
to carry the cane of a lame."
Arthur Schnitzler, Austrian dramatist
(1862 - 1931)

Active and passive listening

There are conversationalists who are very active. It might be noticed through questions posed or interjections, or they keep themselves busy with their own documents, or they initiate an exchange with their immediate neighbor.

The moderator should not overlook their behavior because these people may turn into 'oppositional participants'. Therefore, it is advisable to

- look at
- nod at
- (maybe) directly talk to

the relevant person.

At the beginning of the discussion you should clarify the 'organizational' matters. Among others, this includes how the participants deal with each other. For example:

- by raising one's hand as a request to speak,
- let others speak,
- speak to each other using names.

The typical person – Dynamic of a conversation in a group

Michael Birkenbihl (1921-1993) differentiated the seven following types of participants in group discussions ("Train the Trainer", Verlag moderne Industrie AG & Co, Landsberg am Lech), who are described here as a listener or participant in a presentation. These kinds of characters will crystallized especially in during team-working or group assignments.

The informal leader

If the members of a group need to make a decision, nearly always, one of the group members will take a more active role than other members.

This person will try to present his own opinion in such a way that most other people will agree with him. This person will develop into the informal leader of the group.

This person should not be mistaken with the formal leader of the group, i.e. the superior or the presenting person.

The informal leader tries to compel other team members so that it is obvious that he has clearly taken the leadership role.

This informal leader, we can also call him the informal superior, does not necessarily directly confront the formal leader (presenter). He possibly acts hidden, i.e., not outspoken. He also can send somebody ahead, in order to not appear as the leader himself.

For the presenter this situation is quite difficult because it might take to time to identify the informal leader of the group.

If the presenter has the informal leader 'against' him, it will be difficult to get the entire group to follow the presenter. As described above the group will follow the informal leader. Whatever this person does or says is seen as the right thing and therefore an unwritten rule.

If the informal leader agrees with the position of the presenter than it is easy for the presenter to lead the group. Therefore the presenter has an 'ally' within the group who supports his behavior. It would be sufficient to persuade the informal leader of a group because the rest of the group will follow him anyway.

We realized that the informal leader has a very dominating role within a group. Many presenters failed in their presentation simply because of the fact that they did not realize or underestimated the power of the informal leader of a group.

The competent one

Let's talk about the most proficient one! He also can be a new member to the group who tries to distinguish himself though excessively fast and proficient work.

The group will bring him back to the usual working pace. If it does not work out he will develop from being the competent one to be an outsider.

The goal should be to integrate this person with caution because he usually combines a lot of (professional) knowledge.

The favorite

In every group there will be 'everybody's favorite', who will listen to all the problems and difficulties other group members have and who will try to solve, communicate, or arbitrate.

He also might be the person, who presents wishes and suggestions of the group to the outside, i.e., to the superior of the group.

Usually, the favorite person will not take the role of the informal leader. Affectionately we can also call this role 'mother of the nation' or 'mother of the team'.

This person is no 'threat' to the presenter.

The group idiot

There is still missing the group-idiot. Usually, he needs to take care of all unpleasant assignments.

He does that because his performance does not comply with the performance of the rest of the group, no matter how much he tries. The group will always stand-up for their group-idiot and defend him.

The presenter should not make the mistake of handing this person as an 'idiot' because the other persons of the group will protect him. Then, the presenter would have the entire audience against him.

The opposition

Furthermore, there will be an oppositional person within the group. This person represents a difficult situation. He does not like anything and he is against anything and everybody.

He acts against the formal leader of the group, and maybe also against the informal leader. The presenter will have difficulties in handling the oppositional person, especially, when this person develops into an outsider.

His position will always be against the group and the presenting person.

If it is not possible for the oppositional person to 'conform´ himself within the group the ultimate decision has to be to eliminate him from the group.

But we also should not forget that the oppositional person invests lots of energy and generates many ideas, which also could be good for the subject or the presenter.

The goal should be to change this kind of wasted energy into usable energy for the team or the presenter. If this attempt is not successful the presenter, the other group members, or the audience will be glad, when he is finally excluded.

The adjuster / yes-man

One of the reasons why the informal leader can develop so strongly is because the majority of the group members are yes-men or adjusters.

These people always orient themselves around the strongest person in the group and always agree with him. That is the reason why the informal leader can develop so strongly.

Usually, adjusters are 'nice' people, who try to avoid conflicts. They are satisfied if other people make decisions for them.

There is no threat for the presenter by the adjuster.

The outsider

When a new group is formed, it is possible that there are two potential leaders confronted with each other.

Each of them will try in a tough contest to win over the power. Understandably, it creates disruptions in the way the group functions and; therefore, can result in losses for the organization. Such a situation also can appear if an outsider tries to join a group.

First, he will be the outsider because he is a new person in a group. He has several opportunities how to behave within the group.

In the beginning usually, he will act quietly, and he will try to adjust to the other persons. Once he succeeds this, he will be an adjuster, i.e., a yes man.

It is also possible that he will try to take the leadership role within the group. First, his behavior will be quiet. As soon as he has identified and evaluated the informal leader, and believes that he can outmatch him, he will try to take over his position.

It will result in power struggle and disrupt the group. Depending on the strength of the group, the adjuster will wait and see who will be the winner of the "battle" and afterwards follow him as the proven old informal leader or as the new leader of the group.

The third possibility is that the outsider will always be an outsider to the group. He is not able to adapt to the group, maybe the other persons simply do not like him or he has difficulties in integrating.

He also could have violated existing rules (maybe unwritten and created by the group), and therefore, no real chance to be dealt with equally.

This also happens to group members who violated some sort of rules and therefore were ostracized by the group and labeled as an outsider.

By the way: there are unwritten laws and rules in every organization. Therefore, it is difficult for new employees to find these rules - which are not written down in black on white - to identify them, learn about them, or conform to them to the satisfaction of their co-workers.

But back to the members of the group: The presenter should try to carefully integrate the outsider inside the group. If not successful, it is advisable to try to find a different assignment for him in a different group.

Chapter 4 – Rumor and Guilt

Accusation of blame

"There is no right to laziness."
Gerhard Fritz Kurt Schröder, German Chancellor (*1944)

It's your fault

We can assume that the human species generally seek to blame other people for their own faults:

- "You misunderstood."
- "You didn't tell me that."

Or it is distinguished as an 'advice':

- "It would have been better if you did it this way."

How does somebody feel if he hears such a statement? Self-confidence obviously will not increase though such a behavioral pattern.

In addition, we do not know if the other person understood it wrong. It just seems to be this way from our point of view.

Practice the following exercise: Write in the frame below what is written there as a statement. After that you should continue to work.

THE INTELLIGENT THOUGHT

Did you find the three possibilities?

Presumably not. Usually we just recognize one of the two possibilities:

1. the INTELLIGENT thought, i.e.,
2. an intelligent person thought, or,
3. the intelligent THOUGHT, i.e. the thought which is intelligent.

With this example, we demonstrate how difficult it is to communicate an easy statement of three words with an exact expression.

Of course, the statement is without context and all letters were capitalized, but we wanted to demonstrate with this exercise how easy it is to be misunderstood.

We conclude that it is very easy to have a false impression. And that means that the presenter has to express himself as crisply and clearly as possible. It is possible to clear up misunderstanding through enquiries.

Imagine the following situation:

- Client A says: "Produce (draw) for me a picture of 'THE INTELLIGENT THOUGHT'." He thinks of an intelligent person. In his favor, we assume that he does not know the other alternative and therefore, he cannot recognize there is even a misunderstanding possible.

Now, imagine how the situation might continue:

- The participant starts to produce (i.e., he draws). He understood what his client said: 'THE INTELLIGENT THOUGHT'. Or did he not? Well, he understood the 'THOUGHT'.

  In his favor, we also assume that he does not know the other alternative and therefore, he will not ask any further questions.

  For him, the order is <u>explicitly clear!</u> Therefore he produces a 'THOUGHT'.

After the arranged time the participant presented his work ('THOUGHT') and when the client sees it he throws his hands up in horror:

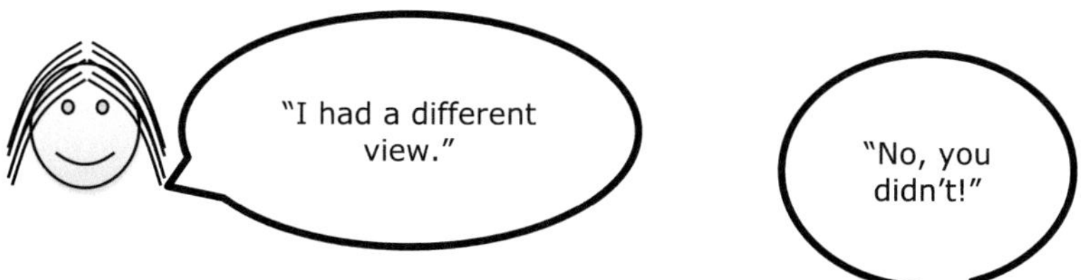

The producer rants over the client's statement.

It seems to be that there is no solution in sight.

Each of them believes that the misunderstanding is the other person's fault and that he is correct. This is a poor basis for a mutual agreement – right?

What is ironic is that both feel that they are right – and therefore blame the other one for the misunderstanding.

With this example, we saw that often there are two, or maybe three right solutions. Therefore a process of rethinking should start. Namely:

- 'if A is right, B does not necessarily need to be wrong',
- 'if A is right, B might be different!'

If people do not label the behavior of statement of the other one as 'wrong' but as 'different', than they both can deal in a more stress-free environment with each other.

Consequently: No accusation or blame. It is advisable to react and orient yourself, e.g., you could say:

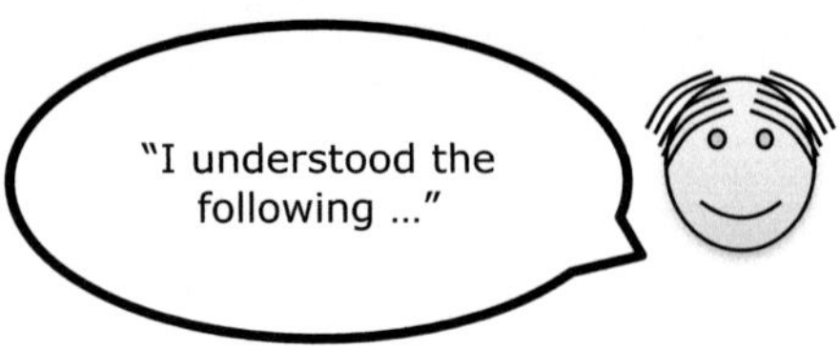

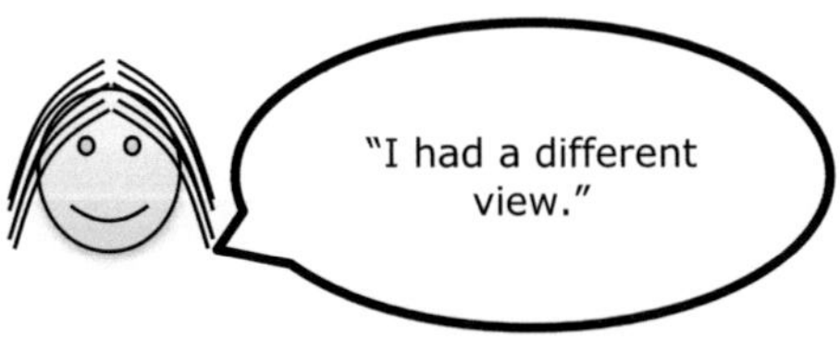

Occurrence of misunderstandings and rumors – Rumor test

Are you susceptible towards rumors? Read the following situation below once and then answer the question (without going back):

> *The chief executive assistant Mrs. Mertens has worked for the corporation for a long time and she is also waiting for quite some time for a raise. She sees on the desk of a superior the drawing plans by an architect. She informs her colleague, Mrs. Nettekoven, that there is money for new buildings but not for the employees.*

Mark as follows:

T = the statement is right F = the statement is false

? = cannot tell in regard to the described situation

The statements from the story			
		R	F
1.	The name of the executive assistant is Mrs. Mertens.		
2.	On the desk of her superior lies a drawing plan.		
3.	The drawing plan was created by an architect.		
4.	The drawing plan shows the layout of a new office building.		
5.	Mrs. Mertens has not worked as a chief executive assistant for very long.		
6.	She asked for a raise.		

7.	Her superior did not approve a raise for Mrs. Mertens.		
8.	Mrs. Mertens is frustrated about the behavior of her superior.		
9.	Mrs. Nettekoven works for the same corporation as Mrs. Mertens.		
10.	Mrs. Nettekoven believes that it is not fair that there is no money for employees.		

The answers:

1.	T	It is written this way in the text.	
2.	?	We do not know.	It is possible but we do not know exactly. The drawing plan lies on the desk of a superior and not necessarily on the desk of Mrs. Mertens' superior.
3.	T	It is written this way in the text.	
4.	?	We do not know.	
5.	?	We do not know.	We know that she is working for the corporation for a long time but the situation does not indicate how long she works as chief executive assistant.
6.	?	We do not know.	The situation just indicates that she is waiting for a raise.
7.	?	We do not know.	Out of the situation we do not even know if Mrs. Mertens asked for a raise.
8.	?	We do not know.	Maybe, maybe not.
9.	T	It is written this way in the text.	
10.	?	We do not know.	

Well, how many correct correlations did you find? Do you still think that you are not susceptible for rumors?

By the way: usually the person concerned is the last one to hear about the rumor.

Typical characteristics of a rumor

A rumor:

- can be distributed knowingly or unconsciously,
- can be based on facts,
- gets distributed in a runaway manner,
- is usually forwarded verbally,
- is unauthenticated,
- is very often strained, deformed, or falsified (e.g., make a mountain out of a molehill),
- gets distributed faster, the more profoundly the rumor affects the receiver,
- is amplified, if missing information wakens the imagination of the receiver,
- is distributed faster, if it is an 'equivocal' rumor.

Helpful communication strategies ... and prevention of misunderstandings

In the following we assume that all persons involved in a conversation want to reach a positive outcome. Therefore, we should consider:

1. Humanity

Create close contact to conversation partners.

It is essential for every conversation, even if there are hassles, to create close contact with the other side and to keep it. Inevitably, the way to achieve humanity is by demonstrating appreciation for the other position:

2. Creativity

Experimenting with thoughts for role reversal. Use your creative mindset; use your right hemisphere (brain hemisphere).

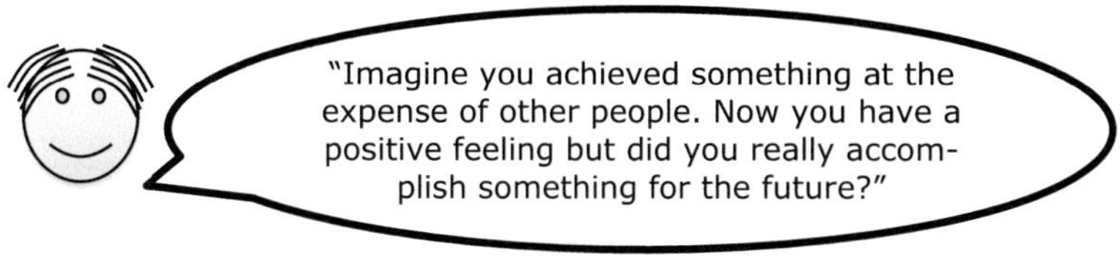

3. Complexity

Broaden your horizon (unlocking paradigm).

Instead of just concentrating on a difficult situation, it might be reasonable to include the complete environment:

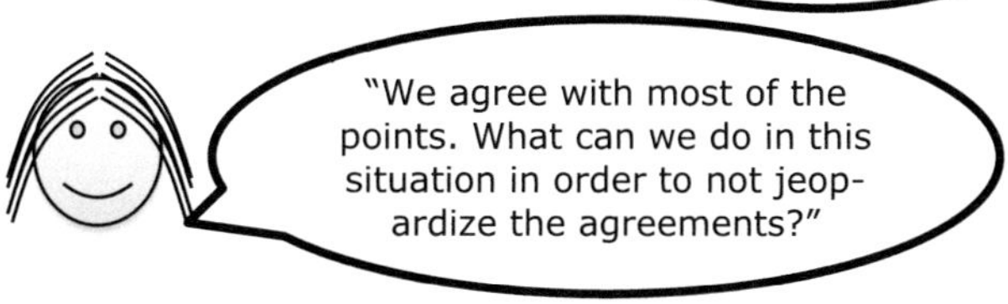

4. Needs

Know and use needs, motives, interests, and decision criteria of the other person (needs-clarification).

- Does your conversation partner think rationally (left hemisphere with right- hander)? Do numbers, data, and facts come to the forefront? Then you should present him his advantage with numbers and data.
- Vice versa: If you want to avoid a certain decision you can argue with thoughts from the right hemisphere. ("Imagine, that …")

5. Wavelength – the 'chemistry' must be right

- Create a good connection.
- Try to understand the world of the other person (active perception).
- Create a good conversational atmosphere so reciprocal trust is possible.

6. Atmosphere

Choose a suitable and fear-free room. Create a positive and stress-free atmosphere.

In an appraisal interview in the supervisor's office, the employee does not necessarily have to have a comfortable or harmonic feeling.

It would be better to have this conversation at a 'third' location, possibly in a neutral conference or seminar room.

An appropriate and strategically sensible sitting posture creates trust and advances a positive flow of the conversation.

Chapter 5 – From monologue, over dialogue to a group conversation

Human monologue

"Two monologues,
which interrupt each other again and again,
are called discussion."
Charles Tschopp, Swiss writer
(1899 - 1982)

"I came, I saw, I conquered" ...

... are supposed to be the words of Gaius Julius Caesar after conquering Phanarces II. at Zela in 47 BC within five days.

Healthy self-confidence or egomaniac?

Nowadays, we usually enjoy it if somebody has self-confidence. We like people who know what they want, and who set themselves realistic aims and then try to reach them.

On the other side we see every day on the streets – and not only in traffic, also in shopping malls – egoism more and more. The impression could mean that only

- the first,
- the best,
- the fastest, etc.

can survive within our society.

Actually, that might be true. I agree, we like to be surrounded by winners, otherwise celebrities and stars would not have so much attention.

On the other side, we do like people who respect human needs and those who try to reach their aims in consideration of others.

Thus, we are somehow in a predicament: On one side self-confident behavior and on the other side not to act too egoistical.

The author prefers the wording: healthy egoism. This formulation is a combination of a well-developed self-confidence and healthy egoism.

Of course, we try to belong to the group of winners but it does not necessarily need to be the first place. Also the second, third, and sometimes a 100th place might be a great place.

Egoistics only know monologue. Persons with a healthy egoism prefer a dialogue.

What is a dialogue?

According to a German encyclopedia (Großes Lexikon in Farbe, 1993), a dialogue is a conversation between two or several persons.

Is it that easy?

Isn't there much, much more behind a dialogue? To jointly talk to each other cannot be that difficult, right? Well, if we consider how easily there might be misunderstandings then we realize that it is obviously not that easy to have a reasonable dialogue.

For further reading, it is noteworthy that a dialogue can be carried on not only with two persons but also with several persons.

If we look at it precisely, then it always is two-person-conversation between people even if more are present. Then we have several dialogues parallel to each other.

In the following, we will consider several different forms of dialogues in interpersonal communication.

Before I start to talk, I need to be sure that my dialogue partner will speak as well. Therefore, part of speaking is listening as well and respectively being able to listen.

Hearing, listening, active listening

We can distinguish among three different forms of listening:

1. Hearing

I hear a car driving by on the street.

This information is not stored in my brain because this information seems unimportant to me. Later, I will not remember the car driving by.

2. Listening

I listen to what my counterpart says.

Actually, I am just waiting for the possibility to reply or answer and I am already putting my response together in my thoughts.

I give my counterpart limited attention and therefore, the result might include misunderstandings because we did not understand each other *correctly.*

3. Active listening:

I actively listen.

For every statement by my counterpart, I try to understand *why* he said what he said. What is behind his statement?

I try to *understand* him. My aim is to sympathetically listen without sending signals of displeasure.

I have the following questions for myself:

- Is it possible that whatever I actively listen to, first affects me neutrally without being directly evaluated or assessed?
- Do I already agree or disagree through visible nodding or shaking my head during the speech of my counterpart?
- Do I have the willingness to accept the opinions of my counterpart without labeling his opinion as being *wrong?* Do I generally accept different opinions?

Reciprocal respect within a dialogue

We presume that we want to come to a common result through a dialogue.

In order to reach a reasonable result we need to see our counterpart as equally human. In every form of dialogue, we confirm:

- I show respect
    - It is not enough to just accept my counterpart – I try to empathize with the thoughts and points of view of my counterpart.
- I am open
    - I am open to new, different, and even ideas contradictory to my own.
    - I open myself to new thoughts, ideas, and opinions.
- I am honest
    - I expect that my counterpart does not lie to me. Therefore, I am honest as well.
    - I express what really affects or depresses me in a correct manner.
    - I act naturally.
    - I avoid acting vain or arrogant.
    - I have no need to make a show by using foreign words, of including intellectual games within a dialogue, or by referring to higher authorities.
    - I do not need to openly or hiddenly threaten.
    - I do not build up hostility.
- I am interested
    - I do listen attentively an actively and will ask sincere questions to continue.

- I avoid questions with obscure statements or accusations of blame.
- I also do not have hidden weapons or strike on open wounds.
- I am open-minded and inquiring towards the opinions my counterpart brings into the dialogue.

▪ I will use all five senses to present

- My goal is that my counterpart understands exactly what I want to present. Therefore, I explain my thoughts instead of just presenting results.
- I present my own thoughts and describe my assumptions and explain the emerging advantages resulting out of these thoughts.
- I acknowledge the sources and pay attention that my positions are built appropriately on that basis.

- I use all five senses in my discussion so that my counterpart can clearly and pictorially understand me.

▪ I think about my statements

- When I want to say something, I look where the incentive comes from to say what I intend to say.
- I consider what kind of motivation comes through my impulse.
- I explain my motives.
- I decide whether I really want to express my opinion or not.
- I consider that my opinion could be in conflict with the opinion of my counterpart. I remain open for other opinions.
- I think about if I can explain to my counterpart how I developed this particular opinion.

- I observe myself
    - During an entire dialogue, I always try to observe myself from outside.
        - How does my counterpart view me?
        - Does he understand what I mean?
        - Do I signal negative body language?
        - How does my communication proceed–verbal, as well as nonverbal – undisturbed?
- I always let my counterpart finish speaking
    - I do not interrupt my counterpart.
    - I listen attentively and interested; let him finish speaking.
    - I take in consideration that every conversation participant has the right to express his opinions and that he needs the same amount of time, which I need.
    - I allow my counterpart to have the right to inquire or to dig deeper.
- I move dull conversations along
    - I introduce a (provocative) subject into discussion.
    - I ask about the experience of my counterparts.
    - I introduce examples.
    - I let my counterpart estimate something.
        - "What do you think how many ..."
    - I ask my counterparts for their opinion.

If we always try to follow these rules within a dialogue, than our dialogues should proceed almost aggression-free and should develop goal-oriented. We can communicate stress-free and successfully with each other.

Dialogue technique

Dialectics means dialogue technique (from the Greek word diálogos). This entails for example:

- I listen attentively.
- I don't have to object immediately.
- I distinguish between objective facts and personal opinions.
- Supposedly, only 10% of sympathy is generated on the rational level and 90% on the emotional level.
- I provide examples (I make my topic 'visual').
- I steer by means of questions instead of statements.

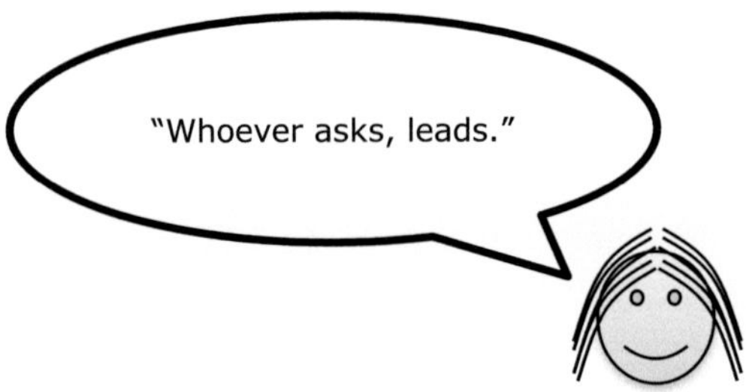

- I emphasize what the two sides have in common (especially in case of differences in opinion.)
- I clarify the terms (define).
- I quote.
- I cite statistics if applicable.
- I don't use foreign words, and if I do, I translate them for my listeners.

Different forms of a dialogue – From monologue to dialogue

Now, we analyze the different forms of a dialogue.

Monologue

One person speaks to a second one.

The hierarchy is clearly transparent.

The person speaking demonstrates dominance.

Feedback is not possible and undesired.

It conforms to the 'parent-ego vs. child-ego' of the transactional analysis.

Typical example: news on TV, severe lecture:

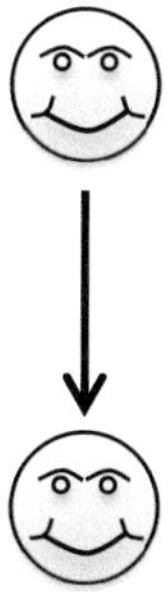

Dialogue

One person speaks with another person.

The hierarchy is not necessarily transparent.

Both parties demonstrate equality: they are sitting equally opposed.

Continual feedback is possible and expected.

It is seen as 'parent-ego vs. parent-ego' behavior pattern within the transactional analysis.

Typical example is a real sales conversation (one person tries not to short-change the other one).

The dialogue can take place with different counterparts in parallel.

Speech

One person speaks <u>to</u> several persons.

The hierarchy is clearly transparent.

The speaking person shows clearly his dominance (e.g., by using a microphone).

Feedback is not possible and undesired.

It conforms to the 'parent-ego vs. child-ego' of the transactional analysis.

Typical example: news on TV, dictation, sermon.

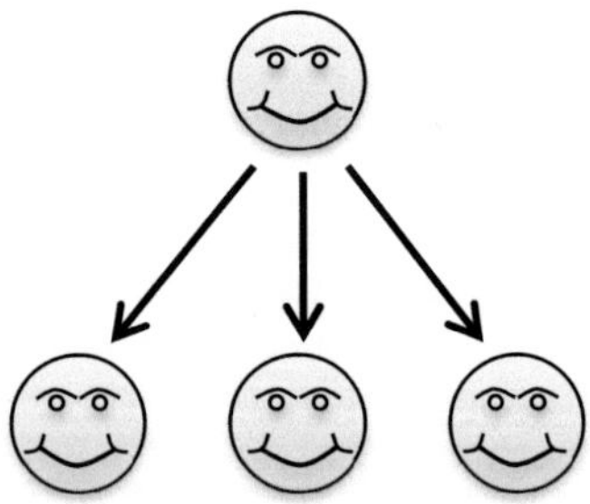

Debate

Several persons speaking with everybody else.

Hierarchy does not matter anymore.

All participants demonstrate equally.

Continual feedback is exchanged among each other.

Candor is expected and is prerequisite.

It is seen as 'parent-ego vs. parent-ego' behavior pattern within the transactional analysis.

Typical example: teamwork.

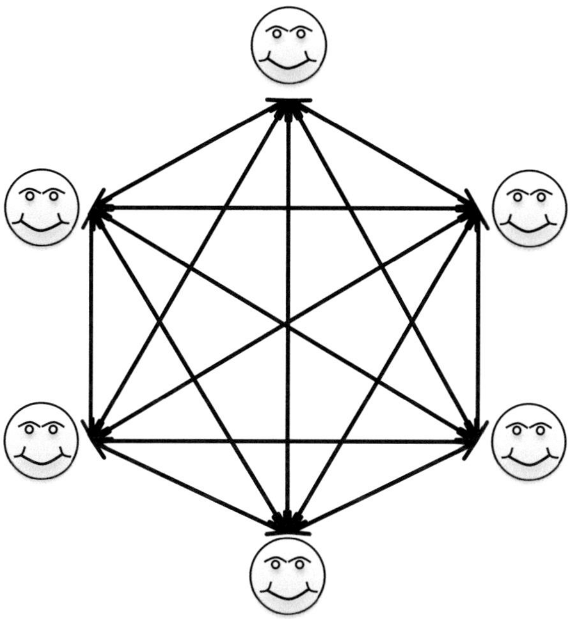

Conversation leadership – Conversation leader

Are you the discussion leader, the moderator, or the leader of the conversation within a discussion?

Let us look into TV-programs and we will see a multiplicity of different exchanges, such as:

- round-table discussion
- moderation rounds
- talk shows
- other exchanges

All listed have something in common in that they have a conversation leader.

A person who leads or moderates a conversation as well as regulates it so that the conversation reaches its aim at the end is called a moderator.

Beside human behavior and psychological basic knowledge, this person will prepare himself for the subject of the conversation, and has practiced verbal and non-verbal communication skills.

And last, but not least, a serious conversation leader is neutral, nonpartisan, and unprejudiced!

Every day media presents us an uncountable number of moderators. The goal of this book is to point out how the moderator behaves best.

Moderation – discussion – roundtable

In the following, we examine three different forms of conversational situations: moderation, discussion and roundtable.

1. Moderation

The characteristic of a moderation round is that all participants are supposed to reach a goal set before the conversation round.

2. Discussion

In a discussion two or even more different opinions are argued by the participants.

The goal is to listen to the different opinions and, as the case may be, conclude in a compromise.

3. Talk roundtable, or round

In a roundtable several topics are discussed.

There must not be a pro or contra and a collective conclusion or compromise is not necessary.

The participants inform, e.g., about their experiences, knowledge, or themselves.

All these situations have in common that:

- there is a moderator or discussion leader and
- that there are several guests invited: a number of five guests is most favorable because
- everybody should be able to present their position without time pressure,
- in case of votes, there is no tie vote and
- there are normally enough different opinions.

Rules of a conversational discussion

Inform your guests or participants before the discussion about its rules. For example:

- the availability of time
- the subject of the conversation
- the modus operandi of contributions such as:
- how to ask to speak (e.g., through a hand signal)
- how you deal with interjections or interferences

Pay attention to the following points for the atmosphere of a conversation:

- The atmosphere always should be relaxed. This way, creative thinking is possible.

- All participants of the discussion should have equal time to speak.
- The exchange of ideas always should be issue-related.
- The topic of the conversation should be clarified to every participant.
- All participants should be able to introduce and express their own opinions, even if they seem to be unorthodox.
- All participants should listen to each other.
- No aggressive language should be used.
- The goals should be understood and accepted by all participants.
- Each consideration no matter how unrealistic it seems should be taken seriously.
- The moderator should arbitrate disputes.
- Different opinions should not get suppressed.
- Group decision can be made through majority. Clear up beforehand!
- Before targeting an assignment try to set a realistic goal.
- If possible, every participant should have the same contribution.

- Every participant should be able to finish his contribution without being interrupted.
- Employ civilized manners and etiquette.
- No participant is personally attacked.
- If applicable, contributions should be protocolled by preparing minutes.

Being a guest in a discussion

If you are a guest in a discussion, you should exhibit (humanly) correct behavior.

We understand "correct" to mean the following:

correct	unfair
precise answers	avoidance, meaningless answers, being a chiseler
no vindications	advocating statements, long apologies
brief and narrow statements	lengthiness, boring the audience
accept statements of other participants	any form of indoctrination, lecturing, arrogant or overbearing arguing
keep calm	aggressive behavior
demonstrate flexibility	advocate, or represent jurisdictional points of view
demonstrate self-confidence and discreet, natural	displaying your own profile too much or too little
request to speak	disturb and heckle

accept the function of the moderator or conversation leader	attack the moderator / conversation leader directly, interrupt him, or question his ability to moderate, correct him or behave arrogantly towards him
let everybody finish their contribution	disturb and heckle
present your own opinion	be authoritative or claim or refer to third persons
be honest	make false statements
call conversation participants and moderators by their names and make eye-contact with them	keep conversation participants and moderators anonymous and do not make eye contact
use gestures selectively	wild gesticulation
use comprehendible language	use slang

Tactic and counter-tactic

Different kind of tactics can be used in a dialogue in order to confuse or manipulate the participants. Following is a short list of tactics according to Rupert Lay and Rolf H. Ruhleder (HMM Hospitality Management Magazin V/2002).

Disruption-tactic

The dialogue partner always disrupts.

- Take a longer break and then ask, if it is now possible to continue.

Layman-tactic

Dialogue partner plays the doubting Thomas and claims that he does not understand it.

- You should answer: "I will come back to this in more detail later on." or "It is no problem, just one moment, please."

Scholarship-tactic

Dialogue partner cites doctrines or (knowingly) cites them wrong.

- You should answer: "But the correct quote is ..."

Generosity-tactic

Dialogue partner claims your concrete facts are imprecise, improper, and inapplicable and so on.

- You should ask him the following question: "What do you have to counter these exact details?" or "I knowingly generalize here because a rough curve can just be explained with such facts."

Ad-personam-tactic

Partner attacks you personally "The color of your jacket fits with your mindset!"

- Attention: In case of personal attacks, always act civilized and do not act emotionally!
- Your response could be as followed: "After this digression into fashion world, should we get back to the subject? "and you should directly continue with your presentation.

Or: Through counter-questions let you dialogue partner repeat his negative declaration several times.

- "I still did not understand you." That helps you to strengthen your position among the uninvolved audience.

Hidden attacks on your knowledge

Dialogue partner refers to contradictory statements in the past.

- In case of an earlier mistake, admit it.
- mild avoidance version:
  - "You see that I've learned." or
  - "I just wanted to see if you are listening."
- cheerful avoidance version:
  - "Well, we can see the world is changing fast. That's exactly what I wanted to say."
- hard avoidance version:
  - "I think like Konrad Adenauer: 'What do I care about my chitchat from yesterday?'"

Generalization-tactic

Dialogue partner generalizes unfairly: "All bosses are the same."

- Identify the generalization and challenge it.
  - "Aren't generalizations out of place here?"
  - "Are all Swedish people really blond and are all Frenchmen really better lovers?"

Competence-tactic

Dialogue partner states towards younger ones: "Your experience is insignificant", or towards older ones: "Your opinion is not up to date anymore."

- The best would be to ignore it and do not comment. Just keep on continuing with your presentation. Or
- Force your dialogue partner to make a statement with regard to his point. For example:
    - "What really is your point regarding my opinion?"

Foreign-word-tactic

Dialogue partner tries to outmaneuver with foreign words.

- Let him define the foreign word:
    - "What do you really mean by..." or
    - "How would you define this foreign word ..."

Phrases-tactic

Dialogue partner is always trying to find refuge in having higher values.

- Directly ask a counter question and let him try to clarify what his objection really is
- After clarification go directly back to business.

Delay-tactic

Dialogue partner wants to refer later to his own objection and keeps on having further inquiries.

- Characterize his actions as unfair and ask him for a direct response.

  If your dialogue partner rejects clarification it is mandatory to seek a personal conversation in the next break.

Confusion-tactic

Dialogue partner uses your expressions and knowingly concludes wrongly.

- Diffuse his confusion-tactic:
  - "I've said the following …" or
  - "I repeat my statement that …"

Diversion-tactic

Dialogue partner inconspicuously changes the subject and introduces a new subject that interests the audience.

- Do not let somebody else remain at the helm. Be direct and civilized:
  - "May I ask you to come back to the subject?"

Either-or-tactic

Dialogue partner sets extremes in acceptance of other's opinions.

- Do not lose control of the conversation.
  - „Naturally there are always extreme examples, but I am sure there is a middle ground where we can meet. "

Major-/minor-point-tactic

Dialogue partner prioritizes a minor point in order to hide a major point.

- Make clear what the 'major point' is.
  - "We are currently talking about whether it is allowed to smoke in church during a service.

    I agree that you are allowed to drink cognac and smoke a cigar while praying in front of your fireplace. But let's get back to the point …"

Discussions

Within a discussion, there are at least two clearly existing different opinions.

Both opinions need to be listened to and their statements must be illuminated. Such a discussion can get pretty heated.

Therefore, it is important that the leader of the discussion round keeps it cool.

It might be difficult, but as a leader of a discussion, you neither express your own opinion nor comment on other person's opinions. ("I think it's great.")

Note: As the leader of a moderation or discussion you clearly can criticize the behavior of a conversation participant ("I believe it's not fair that you always interrupt other participants!"), but not the statements of a participant ("I think your comment is not plausible.").

In order to make the discussion pictorial clear, both parties are most likely seated opposite of each other.

Good discussions arise in combinations of '2 vs. 2' or '3 vs. 3' conversation participants.

Example of a discussion round

Alternative A.

After welcoming the participants, one participant of party A is asked to share his opinion.

Then a participant of party B will express his (most likely different) opinion.

Then again, somebody from party A, then one from party B, alternating each time.

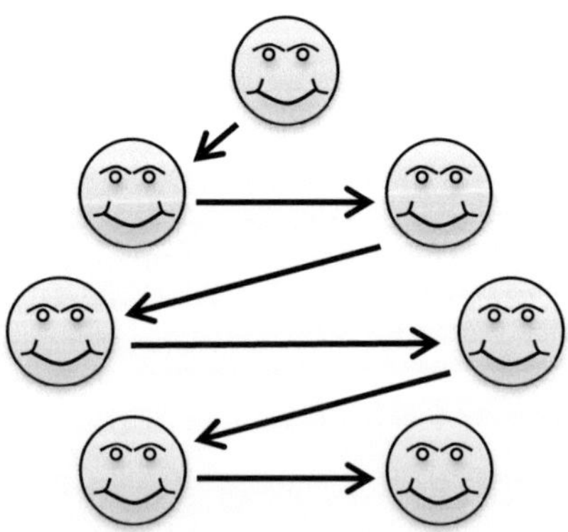

Alternative B.

After welcoming the participants, every conversation participant of party A argues his opinion and afterwards every participant of party B does the same.

With this procedure, the discussion leader needs to pay attention that none of the participants starts to have never-ending monologues.

Changing the contributor needs to be frequent and agile.

Sometimes it is possible that a short dialogue develops between a participant of party A and party B.

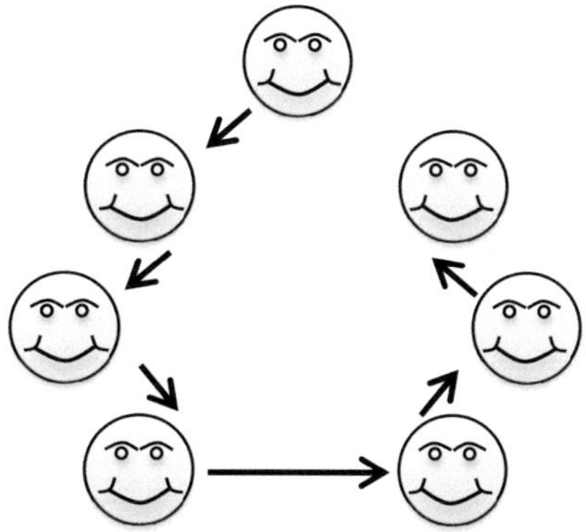

A short dialogue is acceptable. If the dialogue extends longer, the discussion leader needs to interrupt and ask another participant for a contribution.

At the end of the discussion, the discussion leader recapitulates the development and achievement of the discussion.

Talk-round

The guests are sitting in a circle and one after another, one is asked about their opinion about a certain subject.

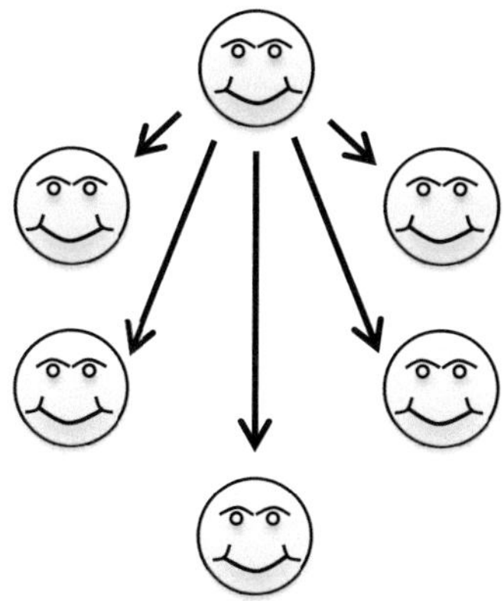

An exchange of opinion among each other is desired.

Also short dialogues in between two guests may develop out of the subject.

At the end of a talk, the guests should have an even number of contributions like in other conversations.

It is not necessary for the leader to summarize the conversation at the end of the discussion because the information contributed by the different guests is usually too wide and there is no mutual goal to reach.

For the audience such a discussion might be interesting if the guests reveal different viewpoints and information about themselves.

Political talk

Very often, it seems like politicians spend more time in television discussion groups than in parliament.

Political decision makers use the opportunity to impart their ideas to the public.

The procedure is the same as in a talk-round.

The guests are sitting in a circle and one after another, one is asked about their opinion.

The moderator does not necessarily pay attention to the fair balance of the contributions.

Debate

In a debate there are two rivals, who are guided through their (conflicting) conversation by a moderator.

The moderator pays attention that both participants have most likely the same amount of contributions.

TV debate

Two rivals meet other and are guided though the debate by a moderator.

It is also typical to lead a political debate with the presiding Chancellor or President and the challenging candidate (in Germany so-called 'Elephant-round').

Both candidates have to either stand up or sit.

There are two models on how a TV debate proceeds:

90-60-30-procedure-model

	The moderator asks one of the candidates a question.	
90 seconds	The candidate answers the question.	Answer
60 seconds	Candidate B responses to the answer of candidate A.	Rebuttal
30 seconds	Candidate A gets a chance to finish the subject.	Response

Town-hall-conversation-model

Before broadcasting, the candidates turn in a list of questions the moderator is allowed to ask the candidate.

Both candidates are standing defenseless in front of the camera.

The moderator interrupts the candidates deliberately, even in the middle of a sentence, if the allotted speaking time is over.

Moderation of conversations

"It's not important that friends get together.
But it's important that they agree
with each other."
Johann Wolfgang von Goethe, German poet
(1749 - 1832)

To open a conversation round

It is time. All guests are seated and maybe there are even nameplates in front of them.

As the moderator, you open the conversation round:

1. You should welcome all participants.
2. Introduce yourself.
3. Define the subject.
4. If necessary, explain the rules of the conversation.
5. Introduce your guests.
6. Open and begin the conversation round.

At the end should finish the conversation round as follows:

1. Recapitulate the conversation topics and maybe summarize them again.
2. Outline results, agreements, and goals.
3. Thank all your participants.
4. Point out further related events.
5. Say good-bye to your participants.

After a successfully accomplishing your moderation you should get to the last part of your conversation round: the closing.

Recapitulation

It would be unfortunate and would undermine your success if you would finish the conversation with:

The final part of a conversation needs a short recapitulation.

The participants are reminded of the main points of the conversation through the recapitulation and they also get an overview of what was said; a quick run-through so to speak.

In order to jog the memory of the participants it is advisable to recapitulate in chronological sequence.

Now, all participants can go home. Hopefully, they all learned some new useful information.

Chapter 6 – Models for leading discussions

Moderation round / the five-phases-model

"A boss has to be bossy."
Jacques René Chirac, French politician (1932 – 2019)

Five phases of a conference

Sit down with your guests in a circle. A circle gives you and your guests the best opportunity to see each other and to directly talk to each other.

A moderation round should reach one common goal, and the procedure to reach this goal is accepted by all participants.

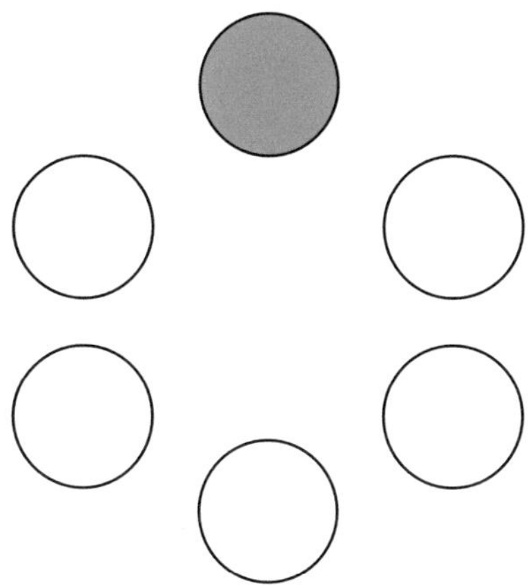

The five-phases-model is a proper way to reach the goal. To set up and conduct (problem solving) conferences, the following stages of the problem solving process are most common.

It is separated into five phases:

Setting realistic goals

Goals are set realistically if they are

- exactly defined
    - what should be reached
    - when do we need to reach the goal
    - and under which circumstances do we proceed
- realizable
    - the chance to reach the goal must be realistic and the goal itself realizable
- checkable
    - through concrete numbers and data it must be possible to analyze later on if the goals were reached
- conforming to the rules
    - The goal cannot be in contrast to the code of conduct of the organization
    - The goal cannot violate laws
    - The goal of the organization must be implemented across all departments. There should not be intra-organization competitors.
- personal or team-oriented
    - It should be decided who should reach the goal.

Realistic and unrealistic goal

After the listed points above we also consider

- the following as an unrealistic goal:

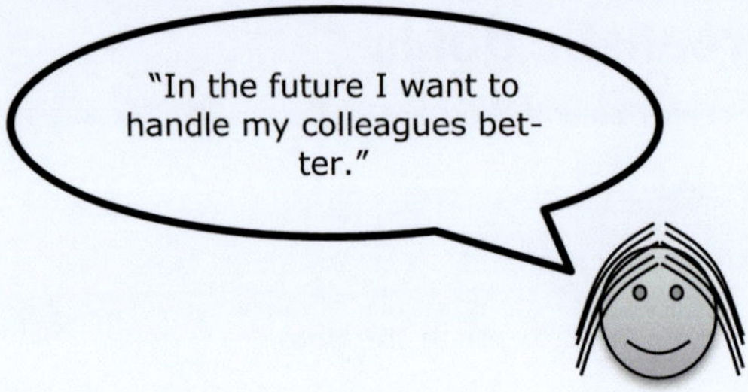

This goal is not checkable because the term 'better' is hard to comprehend and almost not measurable. Beside that, 'future' is not defined as well. Today? Tomorrow? In ten years?

- A realistic goal is:

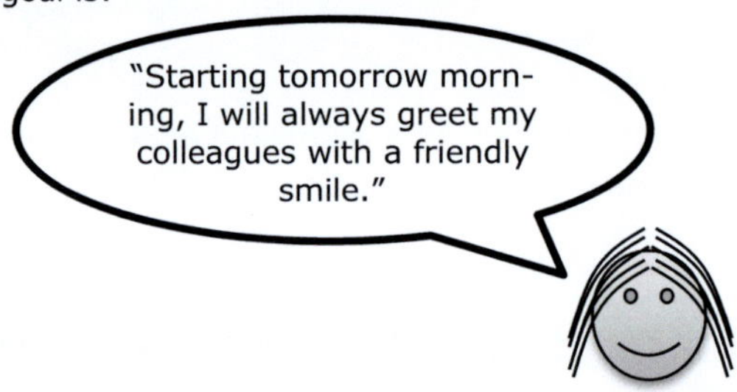

Smart-Principle

The five SMART Goals:

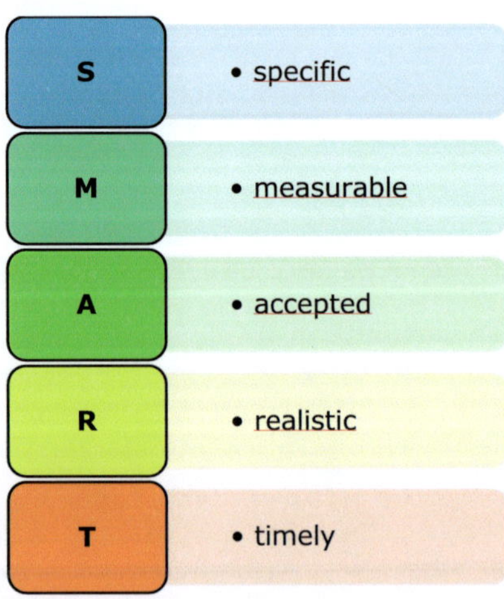

Examples for the five-phases-model

1. Example for an approach using the five-phases-model

Scheduled time: approximately one hour.

The conversation participants are department managers of a public metropolitan and suburban commuter railway corporation. After the greeting follows:

Phase 1: Customers complain about unpunctuality.

Phase 2: Our target is to reach 100 % punctuality for departure times.

Phase 3: Reasons why we did not reach the target yet are:

- automobiles blocking trolley tracks
- passenger are too slow getting into and getting out of the trolley
- bad selection of operating-schedule during rush-hour traffic
- etc.

Phase 4a: Everybody suggest possibilities about how to solve the problem.

Attention: These suggestions should not be evaluated (e.g., through knock-out comments and not even through nodding or shaking the head), in order to not abort other ideas.

- Every participant is requested to have at least one suggestion (sometimes dangerous: "I agree with what my neighbor just said.")

- The more suggestions mentioned the better.
- The more 'crazy' the suggestions sound, the easier it is figure out completely new solutions (nobody thought about before).
- Brainstorming. One after another a spontaneous suggestion is offered; whatever comes to mind.
    - All suggestions are protocolled in minutes.
    - Everybody writes his suggestions on note cards without being influenced from other persons (these are cards in different colors, e.g., in the size DIN A7/landscape).
    - For every suggestion <u>one</u> card is used. Afterwards all cards are attached on a pin board.

Phase 4b: All suggestions are sorted based on priority and therefore pre-evaluated. For all ideas, pros and cons are exchanged and then ideas reassessed.

- It is possible to vote by majority over the reasonable practicality of the different suggestions and about their priorities.
- It is also possible if <u>all</u> participants agree with each other to take one particular suggestion and put it directly into phase 5.

Phase 5: One decision is made about the suggestions implemented. A realistic objective target is prepared:

- who does what and when ...

2. Example of procedure

For an activity of several days. All participants are specialists in one project group. They should deal with the delays in the public local traffic.

Step 1: Phase 1: definition of the problem

- What is the status quo? Where does it hurt?
- Customers complain about delays.
    - They collect data (it is also possible to get data though a customer survey or customer interviews).

- Spontaneous naming of the problems through the participants of the discussion group.
- All mentioned points or problems are collected without any kind of evaluation or assessment.
- The collected data should be recorded (flipchart, memory cards, minutes, and so on). Examples:
  - increasing complaints about delays
  - labor cost too high through absenteeism
  - bad customer service
  - inconvenient shopping
  - assess problems
- Degree, order, or priority is defined. All persons involved decide about the order to proceed in. If applicable, one step after another one gets tackled according to the five-phases-model.

Step 2: Phase 2: goal setting

- Where do we want to go? What do we want to accomplish?
  - The group decides which goals to address (in terms of team spirit preferably with consent).

Step 3: Phase 3: problem analysis

- Why is it this way?
  - The working group investigates the reason for the deficiencies

Step 4: Phase 4(a): suggestion of possible solution or solution process.

- How can it be accomplished?
  - The group develops possible solutions and formulates them into concrete suggestions.

Step 5: Phase 4(b): evaluate solutions

- The group decides which of the solution alternatives should be put into action.

- Experts and specialists can be considered as well.

Step 6: Phase 5(a): decision making

- Which way should we go?
  - Present the possible solution to the executive management so they can make a decision. Then they can tell the team how to implement the plan.

Step 7 Phase 5(b): action plan (realistic goal setting)

- The next steps are ... Who does what?
  - The group decides who and when the goal should be accomplished. The suggested solution will be implemented.
  - Independent from implementation, there will be an evaluation (checking) of the implementation later. The following should be checked:

    - Is there a delay in implementation or are there schedule difficulties?
    - Does the suggested solution path differ from the scheduled solution?

      If yes, what are the reasons for that? (If applicable start again with the five-phases-model). Maybe there is new information gained.
    - Are the known problems abolished?
    - Are there still problems open?

In general: Is just one evaluation control sufficient, or are more evaluation controls in certain time intervals necessary?

Five steps to a goal

In many areas we can use the five-phases-model. Here a short overview:

new challenge

phase	new challenge
1	encounter difficulties
2	localize and specify
3	approach of possible solutions
4	logical effects of approaches
5	further observations and experimental proceeding

teaching psychology

phase	teaching psychology
1	motivation
2	goal projection
3	possible solution
4	attempt and make mistakes
5	enhancement of solutions or implementation

conflict resolution

phase	conflict resolution
1	conflict realization
2	awareness of sentiments
3	ability to express feelings
4	linguistic appreciation ability
5	willingness for conversation

inside management

phase	inside management
1	difficulties
2	actual value
3	index value
4	approaches
5	decision and directive

problem solving

phase	problem solving
1	definition of problem
2	goal setting
3	problem analysis
4	4a: collect suggestions for solutions 4b: evaluate and asses suggestions for solutions
5	decision making, action planning

rhetoric

phase	rhetoric
1	Why do I speak?
2	What is it?
3	What should be?
4	How do I reach somebody?
5	demand to act

Thereby, it is assumed that in order to take an action, the timing of the different phases is as follows:

phase	1	2	3	4	5
in %	5	20	25	40	10

In individual phases, time is allocated as follows: Of course the stated data is not binding.

Brainstorming – Finding new ideas quickly

Time is money. Within a short time period there should be new ideas generated. Brainstorming includes:

- short procedure
- fast modus operandi
- all participants are actively participating
- record all points in minutes or e.g., collect them on a pin board
- ALL ideas have a right to be evaluated

Brainstorming can be separate into two phases:

Phase A. Ideas are collected but not evaluated or assessed.

Phase B. Now is time to evaluate and assess.

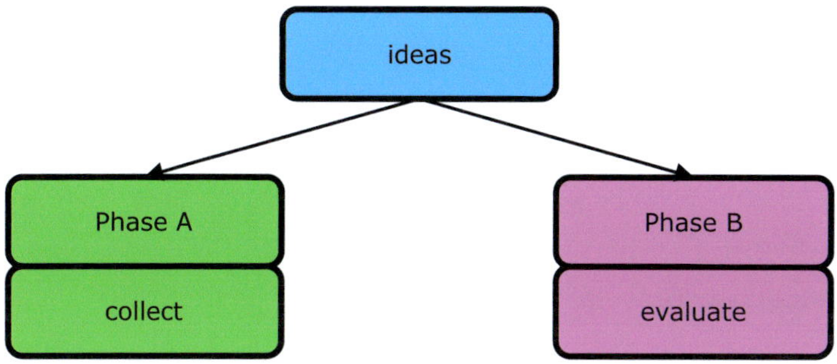

Phase A

- Quantity before quality
    - The more ideas, the greater the chance that there is a valuable solution.
- Everything is allowed
    - Limitations are taboo.
- 'Crazy' thoughts are desired
    - Name all solution ideas. Even if they seem to be adventurous, absurd, or wrong.

- Everybody is listened to
  - Ask in turns around the group or even better use meta-plan (i.e., write ideas on cards).
  - Unproductive and disruptive talk is not permitted
- There is no intellectual property – what counts is the team-spirit
  - Nobody keeps his ideas to himself.
  - Because: Every verbalized idea is a stimulus for the other ones.
- Do not over-discuss ideas. No evaluations, no assessment, or critique at this point!
  - High pace, brief and narrow phrasing: during the collection phase, ideas are just briefly captured.
- Separation of search for ideas from critique of ideas
  - Critique results in blocking ideas. First collect then evaluate and assess!
- keep minutes
  - Ideas need to be written down (white board, flip chart, and pin board).
- Immediately block negative phrases
  - "It's never gonna work!"
  - "How do you want to do that?"
  - "We already tried this once before!"

Phase B

- Evaluate and assess
  - Eliminate everything that is generally not wanted.
  - Stick to everything that is generally realizable.

Specify ranking (prioritize).

Nothing is impossible

Do you think it is right to cut off good ideas through negative comments? Of course not, right?

We characterize negative phrases as destructive (destroying) because they inhibit and constrain us from further (conceptual) enhancements. Here are some (negative but typical) examples:

- "It's not gonna work anyway."
- "It's only going to work this way!"
- "It's not developed!"
- "It was always this way."
- "We can't do it in our corporation."
- "Just try it with our employees."
- "It's too expensive."
- "It doesn't work."
- "We don't have time for that."
- "I never would've expected that from you!"
- "Of all things, you said that …"
- "It doesn't work in Germany (or somewhere else)."
- "Our corporation is too big / too small for that."
- "Your predecessor already tried that."
- "Mrs. X already found it a hard nut to crack."
- "It doesn't pay."
- "It does not relate to us."
- "You'll never get permission for that (from your superior, boss, executive board)."
- "We don't have the machinery."
- "We don't have the know-how."
- "We can't do it anyway."
- "Earlier it worked this way as well."
- "All these modern things."
- "Nobody can do anything about it anyway."
- "Everything is crap anyway."

- "We don't even need to try it."
- "Impossible!"
- "We don't live in the olden days anymore."
- "We have never done it this way."
- "Absolutely not feasible."
- "Absurd! (typical phrases of politicians: ridiculous, non-sense, etc.)"

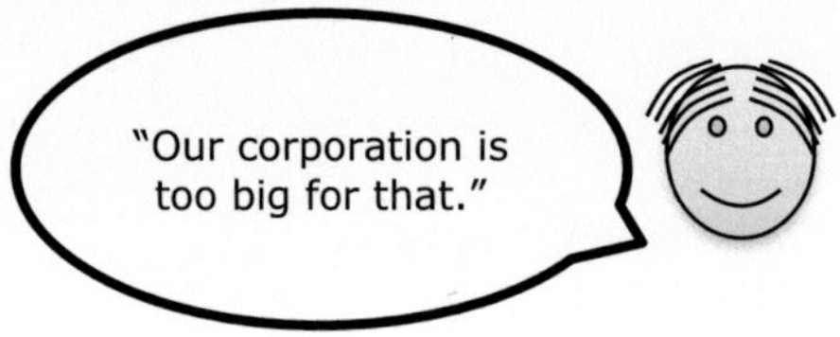

Individual phases-model after having a 'shocking experience'

In case you get verbally attacked by a participant (e.g., a feedback that sounds negative for you) then you can use an adjusted five-phases-model. It will be a seven-phases-model.

Seven-phases-model to overcome a shock

Phase 1: you experience a so-called shock through:

- critique,
- feedback,
- complaints,
- self-awareness.

Phase 2: you negate

Phase 3: you realize a rational insight

Phase 4: you agree to an emotional acceptance

Phase 5: you check it out

- brainstorming
    - collection of ideas and suggested solution

Phase 6: you accept it

- brainstorming
    - Evaluation or access

    - finding a solution

Phase 7: set yourself a realistic goal

- realistic goal setting
    - who
    - what
    - until when
    - where

Realistic goal setting

Several times we used the term 'realistic goal getting'.

What does it mean?

- Express your goal in concrete and clear words.
  - Who, what, until when, where?
- Choose a goal that can be reached through your own influence. It should be realistic.
  - I will ...
- Move yourself mentally towards it.
  - E.g., carry out a great presentation and do not think about possible difficulties in preparing for the presentation.

    If you think about the difficulties it will influence your thoughts during the presentation as well and it will influence the quality of your performance.
- Do not set goals which are too big for you and which could overburden you.
  - Choose a few small and manageable sub goals. Success will be visible faster and it increases your motivation.
- Always have your intended goal in mind (e.g., how successful your presentation will be.)
  - Ask yourself during rehearsal: "What do I see? How do I feel?"
- Avoid negative words such as 'none' or 'not'.
  - Therefore not the following: "Hopefully I won't get stage fright."

    Better: "I wouldn't have any problems overcoming stage fright."

- Write down your goals put the note in a place where "they are right in front of your face"
    - This way you will always remember which goals you set for yourself.

What do I want to accomplish in life?

Example of thoughts about your goal for life.

Set for yourself your own life style. Questions for that might be:

- What do I want to reach at what age?
- What image do I prefer to have?
- What performance do I have to have in order to reach that image?
- What will be the outcome of my actions in 5, 10 or 20 years?

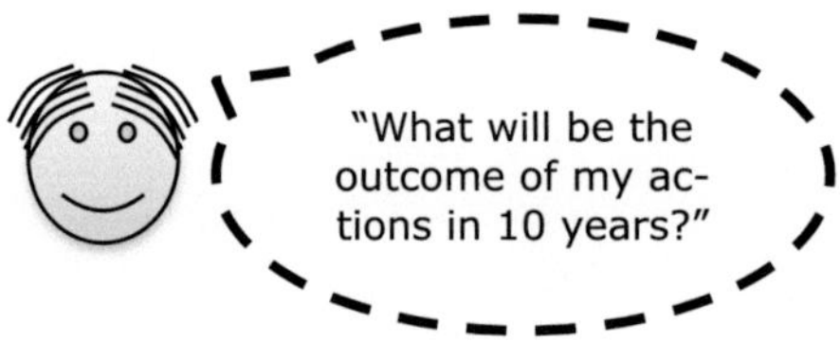

Chapter 7 – Interviews, surveys, questionnaires

Survey on the street

"There is a simple formula about the informational value of interviews with politicians: office multiplied by respect for coalition partner divided by own party minus elector."
Wolf von Lojewski, German television moderater (*1936)

Interview and survey

You have the job to conduct a survey on the street.

Or you want to sell a product. Or – you have the goal to have an optimized sales conversation, a job interview, or a persuading conversation.

In most cases (maybe even in all) it is the goal to manipulate your interviewee until he answers your goal question (that is usually the last question in an interview) the way you want it to be answered.

Imagine you want your employee to increase his performance by 20 % without having a raise. Most likely, he would not agree to that.

But if there is a certain question catalog before, he most likely will answer with "yes" at the end.

Further on below there is an example interview for demonstration purposes.

Do not confuse 'interview' with 'survey'. In a survey, there should be a result without manipulated influences at the end. For example, how many people drink coffee, tea, or juice in the morning?

The result will be evaluated statistically.

Let us get back to the interview. We do not differentiate between the following three types of interviews:

- face-to-face interview (interviewer and interviewee are next to each other (physical))
- telephone interview
- written interview

Methodology

Methodology (Greek: methodos) means: The path to reach something. Therefore, the use of a standardized questionnaire is the path to obtain certain information.

In order to have a reliable average for statistical evaluation, there should be at least 1,000 to 2,000 persons questioned.

Thus, the questionnaire used has to be as objective as possible (e.g., it should include neither suggestive nor overburdening questions).

Additionally, the questionnaire should have the same validity, no matter where (place during the survey) or when (the interview is scheduled), the answers should be the same in any other comparable case (e.g., it does not matter whether the homemaker is asked at 9 a.m. on the market place or in the afternoon at her front door – the answers she gives should be the same).

Forms of questioning

In addition to an interview which can be done with just one other person (e.g., in a job interview) there are public opinion polls or surveys (since George Gallup in 1936).

In addition to a variety of interviews and other forms of questioning in medicine, therapy, and psychology testing (e.g., consultation) which we will not go into detail, there are questionnaires which have fixed questions to be used for diagnostic use.

Structure of the survey

We distinguish 'hard' and 'soft' style.

In order to evaluate the points asked statically, there are several important factors to consider if it should be done precisely. There must be a decision made whether the style should be 'hard' or 'soft'.

- 'hard' style,
  - the focused survey would have many closed-ended questions which give the interviewee almost no room to include his own views.
- 'soft' style,
  - narrative survey with lots of open questions which give the interviewee much more room than just answering with 'yes' or 'no'.

Of course, both styles can be mixed. For the evaluation of the survey the 'hard' style is certainly easier because 'yes' and 'no' answers are easier to collect and count than open-ended answers.

In order to evaluate and asses the response sheets by using the 'soft' style there must be much more time calculated in the beginning because understandably open questions can be answered much a more complex and unstructured manner.

In general all questions must be clear for the interviewee to answer, no matter who asks, and when and where.

Therefore for all questions, there must be a chosen language or choice of words which can be understood by every interviewee.

It makes no sense to perform an analysis on data based on verbal misunderstandings.

Typical mistakes in asking questions

If we use the prerequisite that we do not or, at least to a large extent, do not want to manipulate the interviewee, then we need to take care that we make the least amount of mistakes in asking questions.

Therefore, you should avoid:

- scaring the interviewee
    - If the interviewee is afraid to say, something that could be a disadvantage for him later on, he will not tell you the truth.

      Such a situation could include when his supervisor is present during the interview.
- embarrassing situation for the interviewee
    - Do not put the interviewee in an embarrassing situation.

      Do not ask him about 'taboo-subjects' in society when other people are present.
- overburden the interviewee
    - Do not use foreign words or terminology he may not understand and if it is necessary, explain as often as necessary what is meant by it.
    - Ask questions, which are easy to understand. Avoid nested sentences.
    - Do not ask about a (specific) subject where you know that the interviewee has no or little knowledge of.
    - If the interview takes too long or the interviewee is under time pressure, he might not want to answer at all or gives quick and incorrect answers.

- Under-challenging the interviewee
  - If the questions seem to be too easy for the interviewee, he will lose interest. Maybe he feels he is being fooled. Do you think his answers will be serious?
- Manipulation of the interviewee
  - Many questions can be seen as suggestive questions, i.e., questions that want to influence something. In order to get serious answers, suggestive questions should not be used. Such questions are popular in sales conversations or persuasive conversations.
  - We need to understand that all questions can be used manipulatively. Therefore, we should understand how difficult it is to develop a proper questionnaire that does not influence the answers of the interviewee.
- Surprise attack of the interviewee
  - This is also some sort of manipulation by already making a statement in the question. We call this kind of questions tactical (confusing) questions. An example:
    - "Did the car have its dimmed headlights or its "brights" turned on?"
  - This question indicated that the automobile had lights turned on. But maybe it did not have lights turned on.
- Person and behavior of interviewer
  - We appreciate that the person who asks the questions does have significant influence on the answers to the questions. If an interviewer seems to be friendly he might get other answers than otherwise.
  - Another important point is whether you ask a man or a woman, a young or an old person, how your general behavior is, what kind of etiquette you employ and so on.

Different kind of questions

We classify the kind of questions in two groups:

1. Informational questions
   - Used for information configuration and / or
   - To clarify demanded needs
2. Tactical questions
   - Used for conversation control and / or
   - Used to configure conversation atmosphere

Examples for informational questions

- Closed questions
  - Begins with a verb (introduction to a conversation; target question in an interview; used with restrained interviewee)

  - Answer: yes or no
- Open questions
  - Begins with a questioning word
    - "Where" - "What" - ...
  - A reasonable answer is not possible with 'yes' or 'no'. The respondent needs to explain himself more clearly.
- Half-open questions (cluster question) or multiple choice questions
  - Usually here are some boxes to mark.

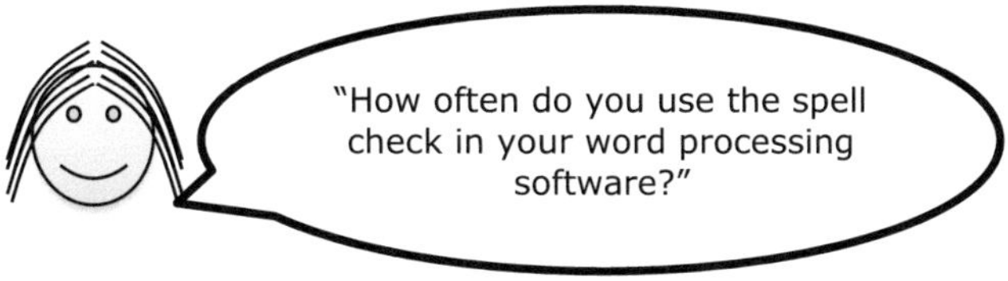

- Possible answers are given: very often - sometimes - never.
- The respondent can (only) choose one of the given possibilities.

Sometimes more than one answer is possible.

Examples of tactical questions

- Rhetorical question
  - there is no answer needed
  - the answer is given by the inquirer
  - during a speech or in a presentation it gets you thinking
  - the audience will be more attentive and they feel included in the subject without a need to answer

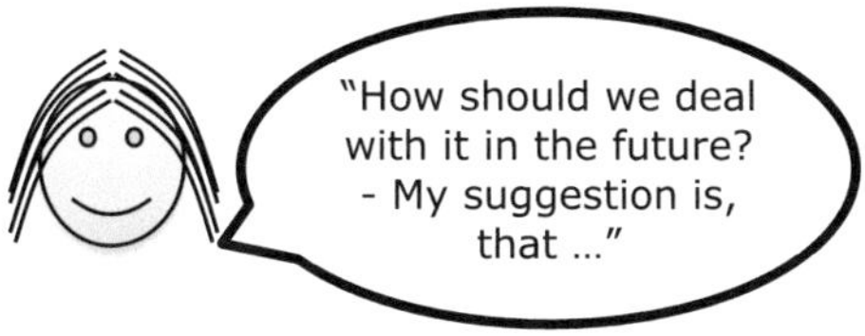

- Counter-question
  - Provides background information
  - Corrects a statement
  - The respondent feels a little bit insecure and asks a question which is replied to by a counter-question.

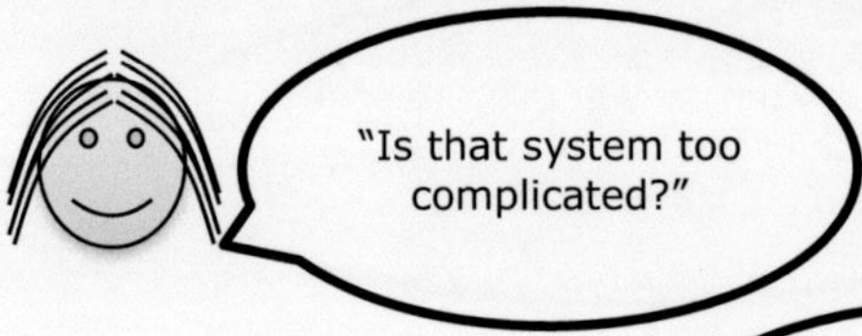

counter-question:

- Suggestive question
  - The expected answer is already interpreted
  - The respondent should answer the question in the sense of the interviewer

  - The respondent is easily influenced

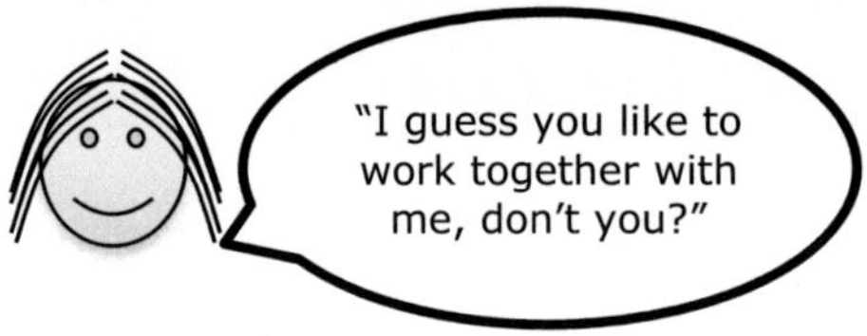

  - Words most likely to be used in suggestive questions are:
    - surely
    - as well
    - certainly
    - right? or don't you?

- Alternative question
    - This is a special kind of suggestive question
    - Two possibilities are given; therefore, 'no' is not a reasonable answer
    - The second alternative (B) is preferred by the interviewer (because it stays longer inside the brain)

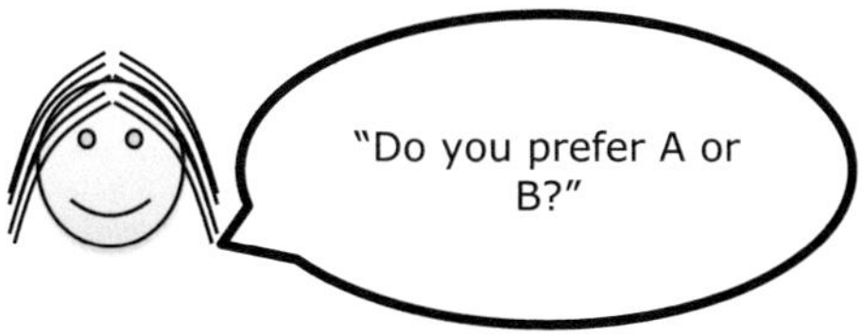

- Yes-answer question
    - It is a special kind of suggestive question
    - Several questions follow each other so that the respondent always needs to answer with 'yes'. Consequently the respondent answers the third question with 'yes' as well.

      After the third question the answer will be automatically 'yes' because the brain indicates that so far everything was right (and was answered with 'yes') and therefore the next answer needs to right again (and therefore needs to be answered with 'yes' as well).

- Conformity question
  - Used for regular check ups
  - Can be used with restrained interviewees
  - It clarifies if the interviewer understood correctly

- Control question
    - Used for clarification; if your counterpart did understand you correctly

- Tactical question (confusing question)
    - Within the question there is already a statement.

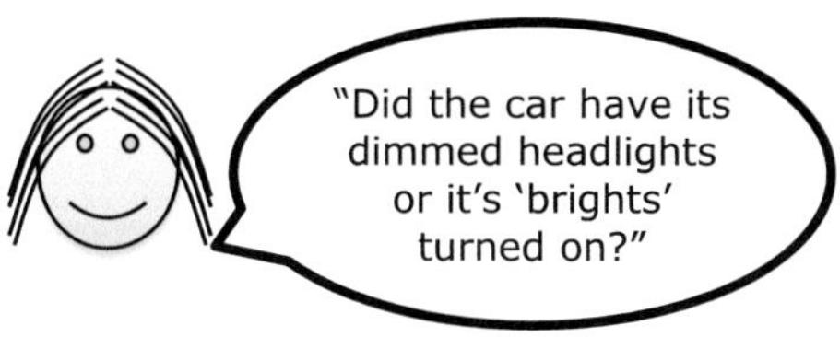

Just for completeness, there non-verbal questions (e.g., through mimicking expressions) might belong to both groups.

Rhetorical question – Why pebbles?"

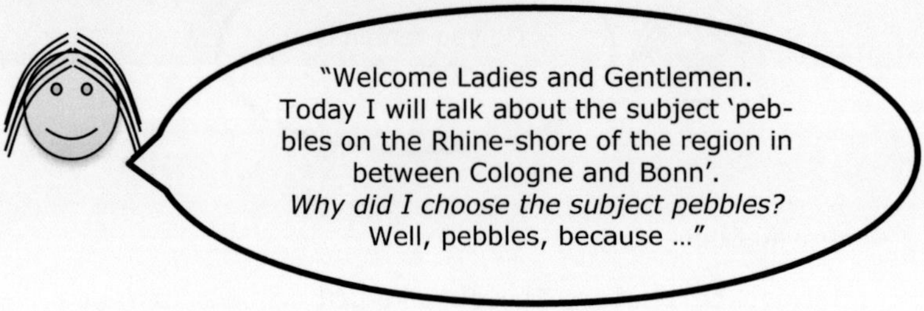

Now, our speaker is already in the middle of the subject. How did he proceed?

1. the audience was welcomed
2. the subject was mentioned
3. a rhetorical question was used
4. the subject was begun

By asking a rhetorical question, the audience might think the following:

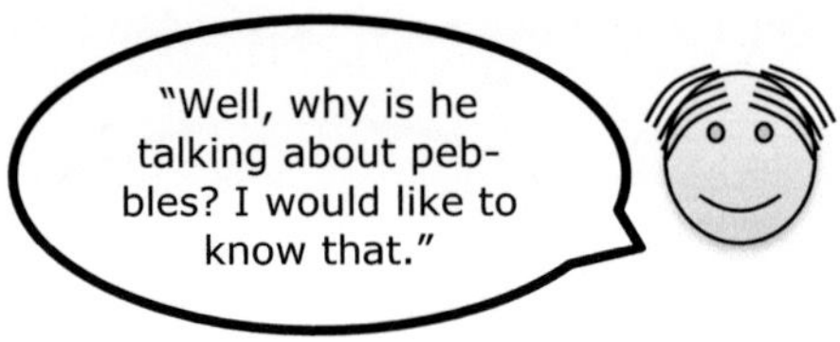

Therefore, the speaker already reached what he had in mind as goal:

- peak the audience's curiosity,
- he them wondering what comes next and
- they are attentive.

Therefore the speaker obtains:

- curiosity
- interest
- attention

These are three important attributes a speaker can use to delve into a subject quickly.

One advantage of using a rhetorical question is that the speaker does not need to expect an answer from the audience. Instead, he gives the answer himself.

Through a rhetorical question, there is an illusive interaction with the audience created. However, the answer is given to the audience in the presentation.

Of course a rhetorical question can also been used at any other point during a presentation. Especially at the beginning of a presentation, it seems like that a rhetorical question is created just for this.

Academic question

An academic question is a theoretical question, which has no relevance for practical use.

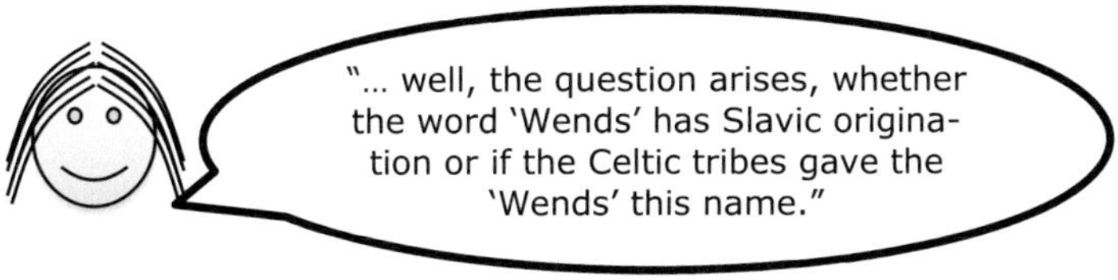

Comparison of open vs. closed questions

open question	closed question

1. Usage

▪ - interviewee should actively be integrated in the dialogue ▪ - interviewee should share as much information as possible	▪ -decisions should be made ▪ - agreement should be checked again ▪ - agreement should be strengthened ▪ - as targeted question within an interview or a sales conversation

2. Advantage

▪ - interviewee has his own freedom for responding ▪ - a positive conversation atmosphere is developed ▪ - trust is generated	▪ - decisions should be made ▪ - time for conversation or interview is limited ▪ - helps restrain conversation partners; use at the beginning of a dialogue ▪ - standardized questionnaire is easy to assess and evaluate ▪ - answers are easy to evaluate

3. Disadvantages and risk

▪ - there could be long monologues ▪ - there could be a different answer than what was asked about ▪ - possible answers cannot be pre-programmed – flexibility about the question is expected from the interviewer	▪ - it could have the impression of a military interrogations ▪ - it could endanger the balance of a dialogue ▪ - can disturb a interviewee and therefore blocks details ▪ - does not give leeway to the interviewee

Question techniques

We realize that not every question fits every situation.

But: who asks – leads; who asks – stands up!

Four different question techniques are usefully interchangeable:

1. open question

- includes information about the complexity of the problem,
- it broadens one's horizon,
- it solves problems,
- it captures coherence,
- asks the respondent to give a more detailed response.
    - Example:

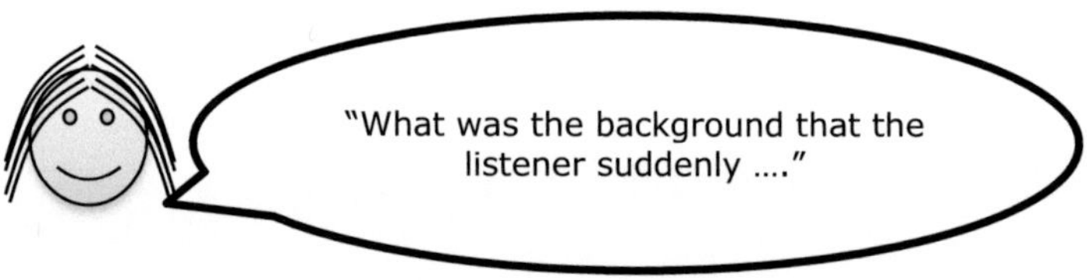

2. reflective question

- reflects / mirrors the opinion, the feeling of the interviewee,
- demonstrates active listening,
- demonstrates interest, appreciation, and understanding,
- establishes a good relationship with the speaker,
- creates respect without giving up their own point of view.
    - Example:

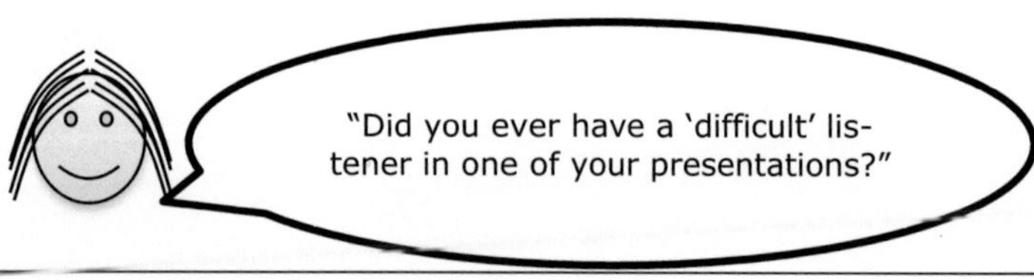

3. trend-setting question

- it is a closed interrogative question form,
- it ask for confirmation of consensus,
- it asks for decisions,
- it shows similarities.
    - Example:

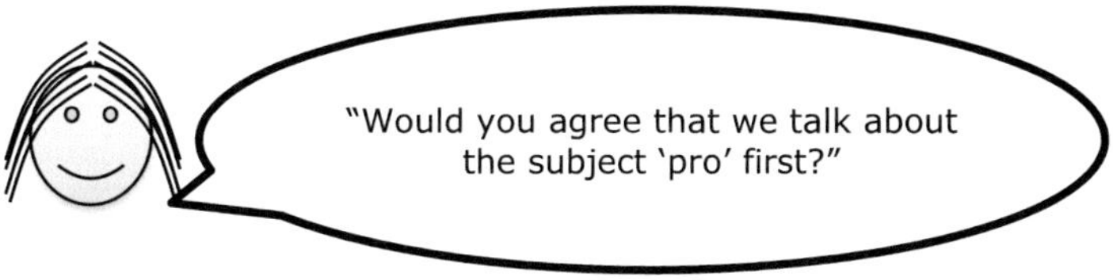

4. evoking (causing) question

- it also is a specific form of the open question,
- it targets expected similarities which are not openly mentioned yet,
- it clarifies the unsaid,
- it asks to find a solution together for the challenge.
    - Example:

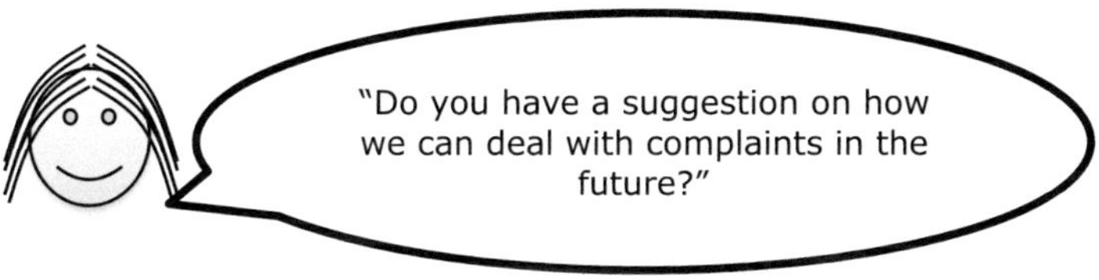

In order to have a reasonable dialogue (if it is possible to manipulate little or not at all) we should behave as follows:

- Make your questions as understandable as possible.
- Make your questions as precise (clear) as possible.
- Maintain eye-contact with the interviewee as you ask the question.

- Give your counterpart adequate time to realize intention of the question.
- Link given answers to the next question.
- Avoid the impression of being in an inquisition (medieval investigation of a heretic tribunal).

Questionnaire

Several questions in a series are a questionnaire. The individual question itself is relatively unimportant in a questionnaire. But the combination of several questions confirms the diagnostic (i.e., that, what it needs to recognized) target. Therefore, the first question should be an icebreaker question.

Dramaturgy (composition and design) of a questionnaire

Dramaturgy is important just as well:

- Ask global questions before detailed questions.
- Overlapping questions with separated options to answer are possible.
- Control questions (in different phrasing in order to check the credibility of a statement) can be included.

Promising structure of a questionnaire

For a successful inquiry the order of the questions is important.

We should consider:

- suspense curve
  - The suspense curve arises from the right combination of questions and the willingness of the interviewee to an emotional commitment towards the questionnaire.
- bumper question
  - In between two blocks of questions it is possible to include a bumper question in order to
    - demonstrate the interviewee that a new subject block is going to start and to
    - soften the possible significant change into the next block.

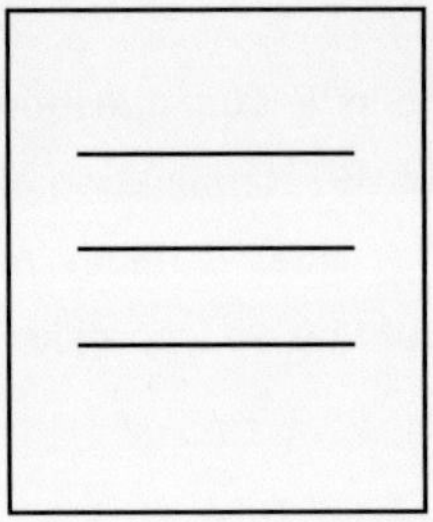

The right order of the questions is the so-called micro-planning (sequence of directly related questions).

That means that the first question is placed before the second, the second before the third, and so on.

It makes no sense to ask at the end of the presentation if everybody can hear or see the speaker adequately.

Micro-planning considers the so-called 'Halo-effect' (according to Gordon W. Allport, U.S.A., 1959), where every question sets an emotional and conventional frame for the next question.

Answers strongly depend on the effect of previous questions. Only then the target question is answered based on the perception of the interviewer.

Each question needs to be in a deliberate order.

If the order is not right, the 'Halo effect' does not work. Therefore the desired result for the interviewer is questionable.

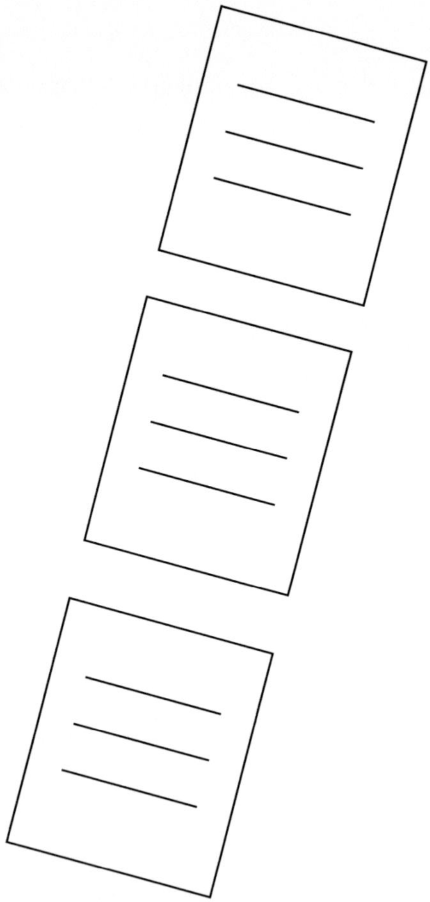

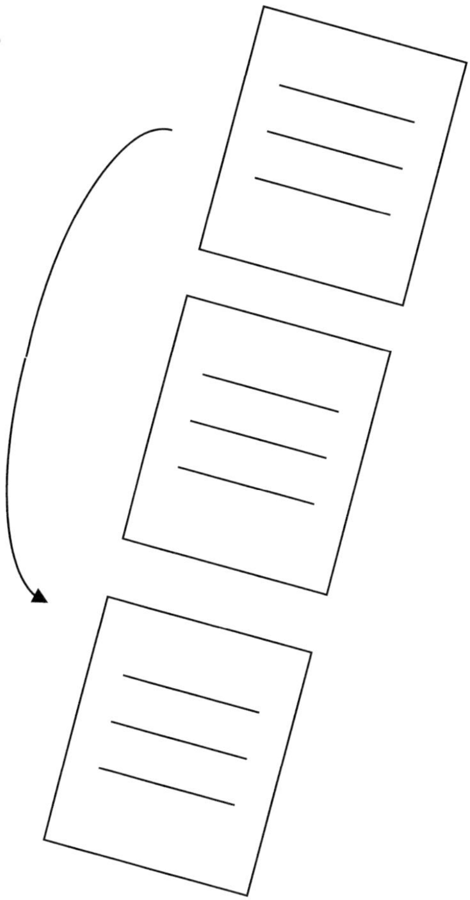

A group of harmonized questions adds up to a block. The sequence of several blocks is a so-called macro-planning (ideal connection of single question groups).

The first block includes the icebreaker question; the last one includes the target question.

A questionnaire logically includes at least three blocks (introduction questions, main body, closing questions).

Depending on the size of the questionnaire, it is possible to use more than three blocks.

On the other side, less than three blocks does not really make sense for a good design of a questionnaire.

The order of the question blocks is as important for a successful questionnaire as the order of the individual questions within one question block.

Through the right order of the question blocks, the suspense curve arises.

In between the question blocks, it is possible to include bumper questions.

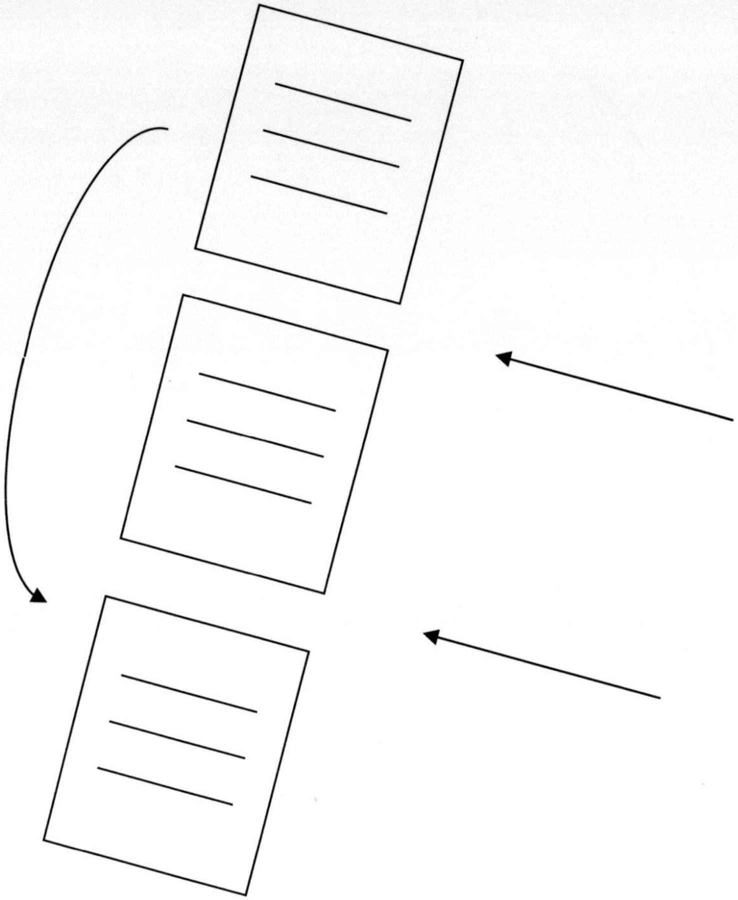

Therefore, the following order of a questionnaire is used.

1. question	icebreaker-question	
2. question		Block A
3. question		
*	possible bumper question	
4. question		
5. question		Block B
6. question		
*	possible bumper question	
7. question		
8. question		Block C
9. question	Target question	

Is manipulation through a questionnaire possible and allowed?

Just imagine: you are the boss of a corporation and you would like for your employees to work 20 % more and at the same time you want them to give up 20 % of their salary.

Do you think it is impossible?

Well, then listen to the following conversation of Mr. Boss, the boss of the corporation and Mr. Mertens, employee in Mr. Boss's office in the highest floor of the headquarters of the corporation.

The 20 % conversation with Mr. Mertens

"Mr. Mertens, how long have you worked for our company?"
"Almost 20 years."
"20 years? That's a really long time."
"Oh, well!"
"Obviously you like here with us, right?"
"Oh, yes!"
"Of course, you'd like to work the next 20 years for us as well, wouldn't you?"
"Definitely!"

"Great, well, you probably have al-ready heard about our problem with our competitor X?"
"Well, yes, but nothing that specific."
"Well, according to uncon-firmed rumors, they aren't do-ing that great."
"Oh"
"Yeah, the Japanese, you know …"
"Yes, yes."
"And the development of the Euro …"
"Yes, of course."
"Mr. Mertens, do you think it's good if employees of the X company need to be laid-off after 20 years?"
"No, of course not."

"I think it's awful. You too?"
"Yes, of course, it's aw-ful."
"Well, you don't want that the same thing happen to our cor-poration, do you?"
"No, for goodness sake!"
"Therefore, you believe that we need to do everything possible so that our employees don't lose their jobs?"
"Yes, I absolutely agree with you."
"Mr. Mertens, I know that you and some of your colleges work long hours but don't you think it is possible that you temporarily work a little bit more overtime?"
"Well ... yes, of course."

"I think that's great and you're really loyal to the company, Mr. Mertens. Thank you!"
"It's all right."
"Let's go all the way! Let's say, temporarily, 20 % more performance?"
"It's a lot but if it helps the corporation."
"I didn't expect anything else from you. Let's put it together: twenty percent more performance, to make it easy starting beginning of the month. Agreed?"
"Yes, that's fine."
"Well, and once we are already talking about. It doesn't make sense to keep on producing high quality goods but nobody wants to buy them because they are too expensive at the moment, right?"
"That's true."

"Taking that under consideration, that our competitor's low prices – in case he files bankruptcy – will flood the market, we should have a competitive price for our goods. Don't you think so?"
"I absolutely agree with you."
"Great, I knew that you'd understand me. Then you'll understand that we need to strengthen our product and in order to do that we all - probably just temporarily - need to accept a salary reduction?"
"Well, yes ..."
"It doesn't have to be forever, Mr. Mertens. However, if everybody here could give up a little bit of his salary, then most likely we are all out of the woods. Right?"
"Under the given circumstances that's obliviously right."

"I'm glad that you'll help us to keep our corporation alive!"
"All right – that's clear."
"Then let's go all the way, right?"
"Okay."
"Well – therefore you agree, let's say to give up one fifth of your salary temporarily?"
"Temporarily – yes."
"Great, Mr. Mertens. It's all settled, one fifth starting ... Let's say starting the beginning of next month. Then we've everything together in one package. Agreed?"
"Yes, Mr. Boss."

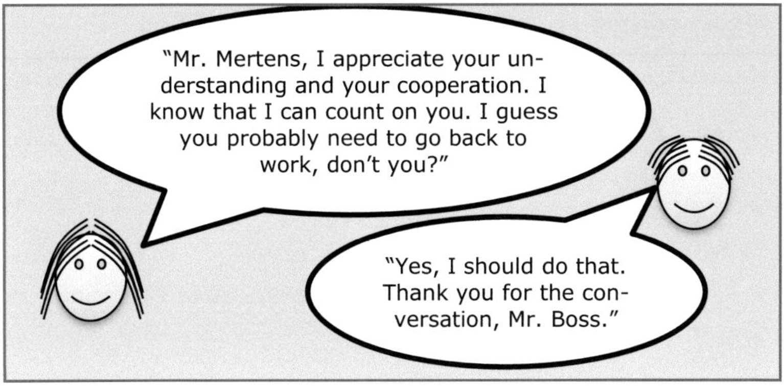
"Mr. Mertens, I appreciate your understanding and your cooperation. I know that I can count on you. I guess you probably need to go back to work, don't you?"
"Yes, I should do that. Thank you for the conversation, Mr. Boss."

What does manipulation mean?

Manipulation (Latin: manu plere = lead with the hand) is influencing behavior in order to gain an unknown use. Therefore, for the use of the person who manipulates.

By the way, since 1945, the word 'manipulation' itself has intentionally or unconsciously a negative meaning.

Manipulation can be used to influence behavior, either intentionally or unintentionally.

- Examples:
    - advertising
    - ideology
    - lying
    - inspire or manage necessity

Manipulation can:

- control the ability of the respondent to make independent decisions
    - e.g., though suggestive questions
- endanger the personal autonomy or independence of the one influenced
- benefit emotional decisions before rational ones
    - e.g., sales conversation
- create questionable mottos
    - e.g., in a sect

A closing remark, manipulation does not necessarily need to be seen only negatively. We also can manipulate somebody in a positive sense – then we normally say to 'motivate'.

In both cases, it is important that the manipulated or motivated person does not have the impression he was taken for a ride!

Bewildering conclusions and others

Do you create bewildering conclusions?

- Wrong generalization
  - arises from wrong reasons or wrong conclusions.

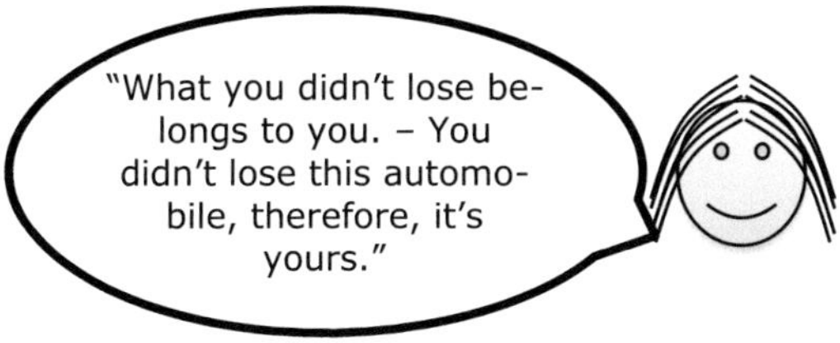

- Wrong conclusions
  - arises from (wrong) connection between causes and effects

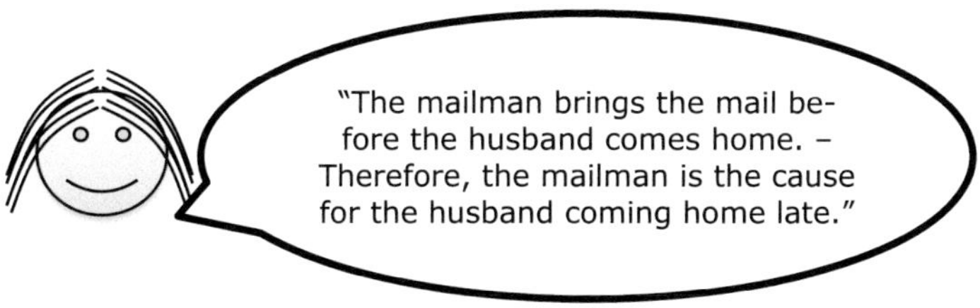

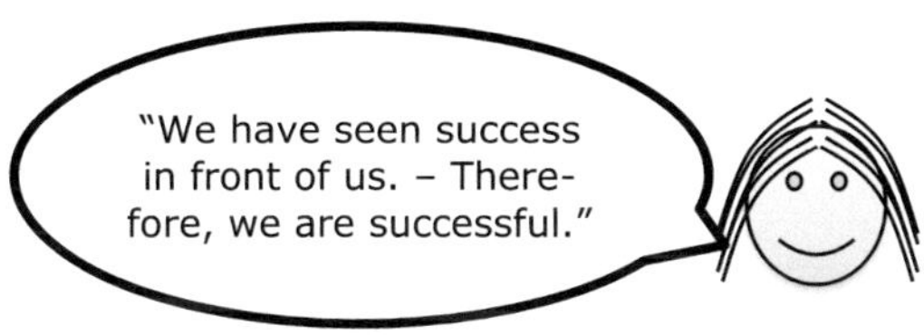

- Bewildering conclusions
  - arise from giving false connection or twisting the meaning of words
    - "Small fry" instead of "young people"

- Insulting addition
    - arises from adding a second word which makes the whole term sound negative

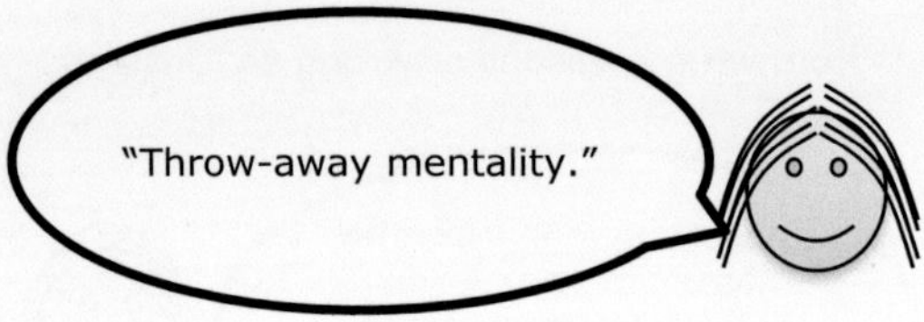

- Abuse of words
    - arises from belittlement of a situation by using misdirecting words
        - collateral damage
- Multiple meanings
    - arises from a word that has several meanings and that is used (cognizant) in one context with different meanings.

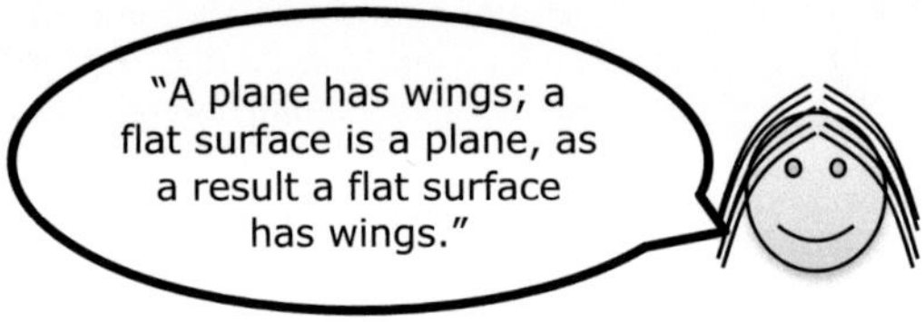

Curiosity is a decoration ...

... but it won't get you far. Or not? Without curiosity, there would not be question. Therefore, curiosity seems to be the reason for a question or an interview.

The form of an interview as we know it today has only been around for one-hundred years. Before that and all the time through World War I German, newspaper people were most likely seen as chroniclers.

Critical questions from newspaper reporters were frowned upon and censors did the rest. During the time of the Third Reich interviews with Nazi leaders where used as instruments of propaganda.

Not until after World War II did the modern interview become common in Germany.

An interview can be called as a "navigated dialogue between two equal conversation partners."

Preparation

Naturally, a very good interview demands for very good preparation. And that means preparation about the interviewee and the subject itself.

Therefore, the interviewer must have thoughts about the conversation in order to formulate the goal of the interview. He needs to ask himself in which direction the interview should develop.

Thus: good preparation is necessary; however, the more the interviewer confines himself to the (prepared) questions, the less he able to be impulsive, alternate or be creative, not to mention be spontaneous or agile.

Leading a conversation

Some interviews sound like a downright interrogation, other ones rather like a chat on your couch at home.

Through proper preparation and a clear formulation of your goal the audience can perceive a comprehensible structure.

Through use of different question styles, the interview seems to be agile. Normally, long questions have long answers and short questions, short answers.

It is also possible to first narrow down the subject by giving a short summary of the situation by the interviewer.

When you want a personal opinion of the interviewee, it is best to ask him directly and use his name.

The interviewer should be sensible or careful about expressing his own opinion because it influences the answer of the interviewee.

Therefore, an experienced and good interviewer will always refer to a third party and explains his opinion. Therefore, he is not framed by his own opinion and therefore not vulnerable.

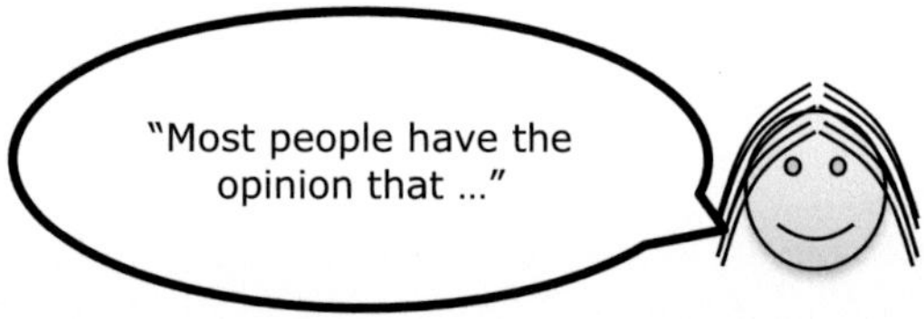

With nonspecific or cagey answers, the interviewer should inquire further. Inquiry should also be used if the interviewer did not understand an answer.

It is expected that if the interviewer did not understand the answer then the interviewee probably did not understand the question.

If the interviewee asks not to publish some of his statements then a proper interviewer will follow this request. It is a question of fairness and trust to act politely towards the interview partner.

Of course, this is obsolete with live coverage.

If they get mousetrapped they should directly confess their mistake and continue the conversation.

Publication of an interview

After finishing an interview, the interviewer will work on the written documentation.

The conversation can be shortened, the chronology can be changed, and it can be restructured. Additionally, certain statements can be accentuated as long as the interviewee agrees.

Therefore, it is best if you give the final draft of the interview to the interviewee in order for him to take a look at it and decide if everything is fine with him or if he would like to change something.

Politicians and celebrities often use this possibility and exercise this right.

And if you are interviewed ...

Never look during a live interview directly into the camera in a television studio. Always look at your interviewer. This also applies to situations where you may get the impression that the interviewer is not listening to you or when he does not look at you.

The reason can be, for example, that he is checking the remaining broadcasting time on a clock behind you.

Beside a live interview, there is also "going live". In such a situation, you are connected with the interviewer in a broadcasting studio through a monitor and a microphone.

Seat yourself or change the position of the monitor so that you are at the same eye level as your interview partner.

If you are asked to make a statement, i.e., a short response, then you can assume that you do not have more than 30 seconds to answer.

Of course, you need to include the most important thoughts inside these few seconds.

Preparation

In order to do a meaningful survey on the streets, it is advisable:

- to prepare one interview sheet for every interviewee
  - in order to evaluate and assess the results later
  - to handle the forms easier (no turning pages over)
  - a pre-prepared form impresses the interviewee
- in between 8 to 15 (as a maximum) questions for each interview
  - less than eight questions: it is difficult to develop a suspension curve
  - more than 15 questions: the respondent easily loses interest
- Keep on field empty for statistical data. For
  - age

    - below 19
    - 20 to 29
    - 30 to 39
    - 40 to 49
    - 50 to 59
    - 60 and older
- Sex
  - male,
  - female,
- Social stratum (without writing down these words so you do not irritate the interviewee), e.g., like that
  - - *** (upper-class)
  - - ** (middle-class)
  - - * (lower-class)

All statistical data should be in the lower fifth of the interview sheet.

Division of the questionnaire

1. question				
2. question				
...				
...				
last question				
below 19 20 - 29 30 - 39 40 - 49 50 - 59 60 and older		*** ** *	others:	place: time: interviewer:

It shall be understood that these details are subjective. But very often they give interesting insights when the questionnaires are evaluated and assessed later.

And one more field – others. Here you should write down unexpected behavior, information or situations (e.g., if a police man is not allowed to answer certain questions).

In case you do the survey on different days and on different locations you should add the following fields into your survey in order to get a reasonable evaluation and assess of the survey:

- place
- time
- interviewer

While designing your questionnaire consider that

- the interviewee will take a look at your questionnaire
- you have adequate space for all answers
- you do not hide text through clips of the clipboard.

In order to compare the answers it is important that the questions on all sheets are the same and they verbally need to be asked by the interviewer in the same way.

Conformity – The experiment of Solomon Asch

Solomon Asch performed several experiments in order to prove the conformity of human behavior.

The result of the experiments was that it is clearly seen that there is social influence on the result.

Humans tend to adopt the opinion or the behavior of other group members – knowing that the opinion or behavior is not right.

In 1970, Asch seated seven to nine persons as displayed below.

Actually, just one person was a real test candidate (the person marked dark); all other ones knew what was going on.

With such an experimental group he did 12 to 18 runs. He showed one test candidate after another (in the direction of the arrow) a card with a standard line on it and a card with comparison lines on it.

standard line — comparison lines

All informed test candidates named an obviously wrong comparison line. The surprising result was:

approx. 37 % - 45 % of the real test candidates	adopted the wrong opinion
approx. 30 %	adopted **always** the wrong opinion
approx. 25 %	never adopted the wrong opinion

Why do we get such a result?

Possible interpretations of such behavior:

- fear to get embarrassed
- self-doubt
- lack of self-confidence
- fear to get excluded from the group
- convenience to avoid a discussion
- herd instinct
- peer pressure – nobody wants to stand out

In an interview the conformity effect among interviewees should be avoided in order to get utilizable answers.

It is time. All preliminary work is done. Now you need to look for an appropriate location.

- Improper survey locations are
  - in the blazing heat of the sun
  - in rain
    - any places or in buildings where the owner can 'exercise property rights', e.g., in subway stations; on patios of restaurants or similar locations
  - In such cases it is necessary to get permission before hand because otherwise it is possible to get a restraining order
  - on locations where great many persons push themselves though a (constructive) bottleneck

Introduction of a survey

The introduction is already important for conducting a successful survey. Many people do not want to answer because they 'fear' they will have to buy something.

In order to not always get the answer "I don't have time!" following are some promising possible introductions:

- Introduction
  - The first question / make a general statement.

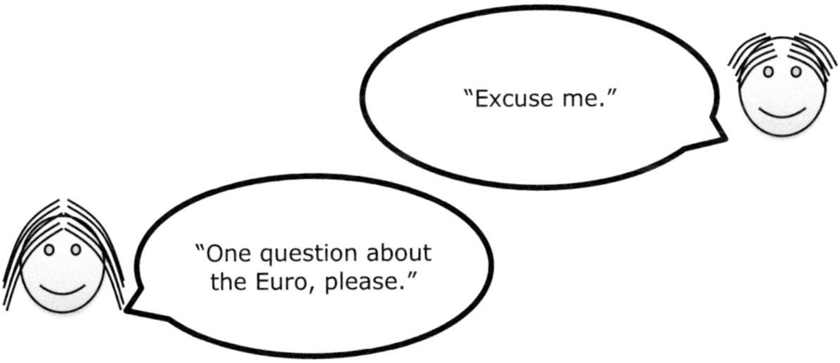

Of course, we will always accept if people do not want to give interviews. Nasty comments by the interviewer are not appropriate and impolite. Your positive behavior makes it easier for the interviewee to answer your questions.

- Behavior
  - smile (honest smile)
  - make eye contact
  - keep physical distance

In case you act as a team:

- inside a team:
    - Just <u>one</u> person asks questions in order for the respondent to become accustomed to that particular person.
    - The other one behaves non-verbal and moves a half-step to the side.

If you meet couples or groups, you need to fill out one questionnaire for each of them in order to be correct. Usually the respondents influence each other during the interview and therefore it is mostly better to just interview one person out of a couple or a group.

Example: you meet a couple and ask one of the persons what the dream partner should look like ... Are all questions asked? Then the farewell follows.

- End
    - You should thank them for the conversation and for the time the respondent took for the interview.
    - Tell him who you are and why you asked.

200 lies a day?

According to Professor Peter Stiegnitz 1936-2017), lying researcher in Hungary, people lie up to 200 times a day.

His opinion is that men say approximately twenty percent more untruths than women because it is said that men speak first and think later.

A child starts to lie with the age of three to five years old, as soon as he realizes that other people are allowed to think differently.

He realizes that he could gain an advantage though lying or fibbing. This is also called the 'theory of reason'.

By the way: in Catholic regions, it is easier to deal with the truth because if people have a bad conscience, they can calm themselves through confession.

Why do people lie?

Obviously people lie because it is easier (and more successful?) to get though life.

- Thereby lies can be consciously false.
    - egoistic lie
    - partial lie
    - heroic lie
- Or, a lie within a not intended false statement.
- And the third point is that a lie can occur because of wrong information.

Whatever motives a respondent has to lie, we, as the interviewer want to hear the 'truth'.

Therefore, we can create through a clever design of the questionnaire a certain dramaturgy to get mostly honest answers from the respondent.

Easy words, easy questions, clear sentences, no foreign words and so on contribute to this effect.

Control questions can be built in order to realize if the respondent answered honestly.

Lies ... or involuntary facial expressions

Basic emotions start automatically. The psychologist and emotional researcher Paul Ekman determined that intentional facial expressions are automatically interfered and therefore uncontrollable facial expressions.

They last approximately one thirtieth of a second and they are not knowingly visible for laymen.

He calls them 'micro-expressions'. Ekman predicts that there are 35 signs that indicate a lie, including facial expressions, gestures, or voice.

Therefore, consider the following: facial expressions are the most important element of body language and will be analyzed by our counterpart (unconsciously but mostly correctly).

The internal willingness to be honest with our counterpart is normally an advantage.

baby 	3 to 5 years 
0 lies	maybe 10 lies a day

female adult 	male adult 
160 lies a day	200 lies a day

80-year-old woman 	80-year-old man 
lied 4,500,000 times in her life	lied 5,500,000 times in his life

Chapter 8 – Manipulation through Statstics?

Do statistics lie?

"The only statistics you can trust are those you falsified yourself."
(pretended to be from) Sir Winston Churchill, British Prime Minister (1874 - 1965)

Counterfeit or truth?

Does that mean that statistics are just in general faked? Wouldn't we rather agree that statistical data can be interpreted in different ways?

The data can be put together in a certain way so that the results can be seen differently. Sometimes we can assume that we can have great faith in numbers. Normally the credibility of a statistic is not challenged.

If a moderator says that the consumer price index (CPI) (basis 1995 = 100) for alcoholic beverages and tobacco products is in 2000 was as high as 107.5 (in all German households; Federal Statistical Office Germany, Mai 31, 2001), then the audience will usually accept that number.

They believe in that number! The audience will not think that the number may be 108.5 or 106.5 instead of 107.5. As a moderator, you can use the belief in numbers to your advantage. Namely:

- the number is said
- the number is believed

Your statement continues

- and this statement is also believed (because the number is already defined as 'true')

The source of the statistical data can, but does not have to, be mentioned.

If you have a source that is generally accepted such as a credible news magazine then the desired effect of the data is considerable.

From this, it follows that, in order to rely (or even to emphasize) on our statement, we include statistical data. Thereby we notice:

- one, two or a maximum of three statistical numbers related to the same information
- numbers with many of digits (if possible round up or down)
  - instead of 3,724,624, approximately 3.7 million is better
  - instead of 0.8769, approximately 0.88 better
- include the word 'statistic' or 'survey'

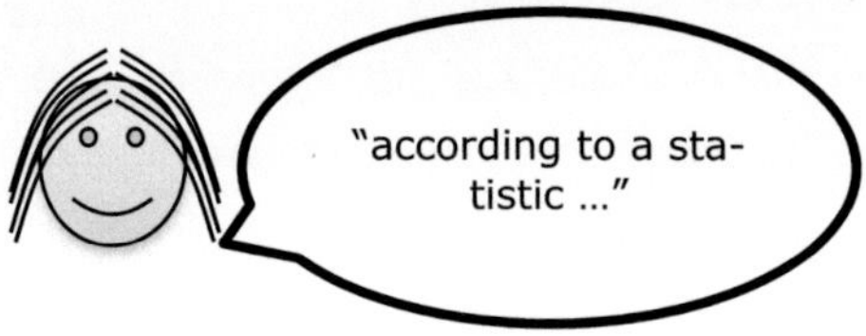

or

- References only if the source is credible
- statement may sound funny to the audience

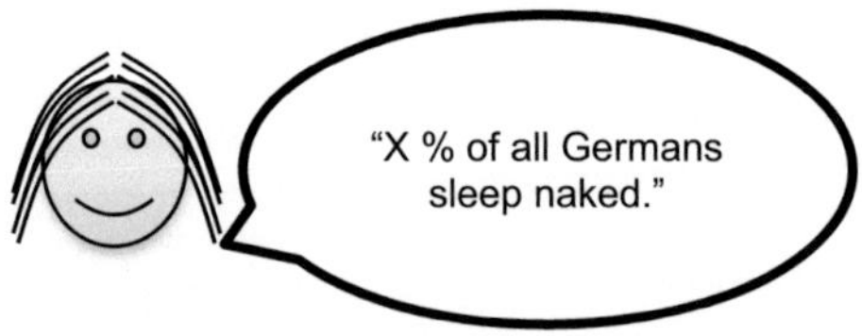

Analysis of the collected data

In statistics, the following terms are used:

- Midpoint
    - The midpoint is the sum of all values divided by the number of single values (of the interviewees).
- Median
    - The median halves the collection of data after the number of single values (of the interviewees) into half-half (50 % to 50 %).
- Mode
    - The mode is the nominal value that most frequently appears.

Example:

Question: "?"

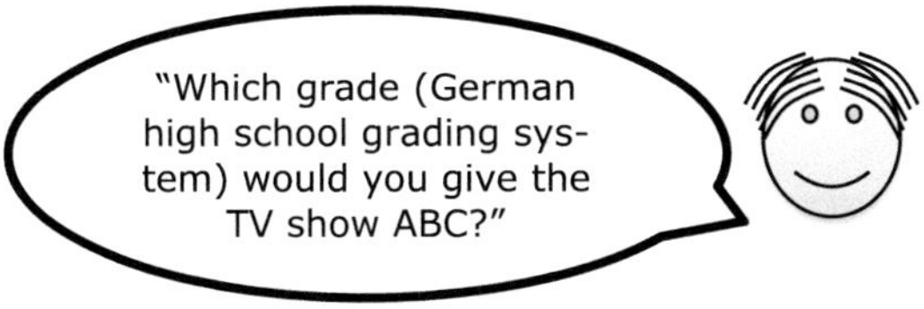

Grade	1	2	3	4	5	6	Sum
Quantity	5	4	7	19	20	5	60
	5*1	4*2	7*3	19*4	20*5	5*6	
Value	5	8	21	76	100	30	240

n = number of interviewees (single value) who gave that grade.

From this table we can analyze the following:

- Midpoint
  - 240 divided by 60 equals 4.0
- Median
  - The same amounts of single value are on the right and left side of the middle. Therefore, we get 4.5.
- Mode
  - The most mentioned value is 5.0.

We see that depending on the used term, we get a number in between 4.0 and 5.0. How we can manipulate with this data is demonstrated in the next chapter.

Real manipulation through statistics?

In the following examples we assume real manipulation. If you, as a lecturer want to manipulate like this, is your personal decision.

More important is that you can realize when a conversation partner tries to manipulate you and therefore you can react. We refer in the following example to numbers which have been listed in the previous chapter.

Result	Statement
1	"Statistically seen there is a midpoint of 4.0 for the evaluated TV show."
2a	"Most evaluations got a grade of 5.0."
2b	"Most of the interviewees (35 out of 60) gave the TV show a good grade (in between 1.0 and 4.0)."
3a	"Half of the interviewees gave the TV show a grade in between 1 and 4.5."
3b	"Half of the interviewees gave the TV show a grade in between 4.5 and 6."
4a	"At least 26.6 % (16 out of 60) of the interviewees gave the TV show a grade in between 1 to 3."
4b	Only ¼ (16 out of 60) of the interviewees gave the TV show a grade in between 1 to 3."
5a	"41.6 % (25 out of 60) of the interviewees gave the TV show a grade in between 5 to 6."
5b	"Almost half of the interviewees (25 out of 60) gave the TV show a grade in between 5 and 6."
6a	"Only 5 persons gave the TV show a grade of 6."
6b	"Almost 10 % (exactly 8.33 %) gave the TV show a grade of 1."
6c	"At least every twelfth person gave the TV show a grade of 1."

Do not forget: The same data was used.

Practice tip: look for any statistical data. Use the numbers on one hand to strengthen a statement and on the other hand for a negative interpretation of the subject.

Smart display of the results?

Due to an (fictional) survey the following result occurred:

in favor	15
neutral	55
against	30

How can you present the result (without lying)?

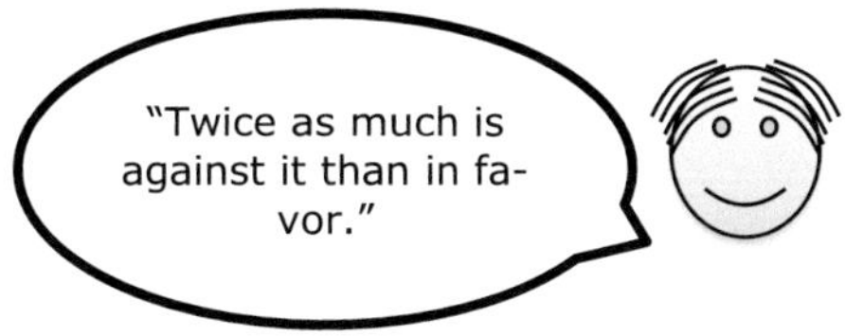

Independent of the data, every statistical number can be used positively as well as negatively.

(Fictional) example:

- Ten percent of all people living in Cologne agree with solution A.

Interpretation and display:

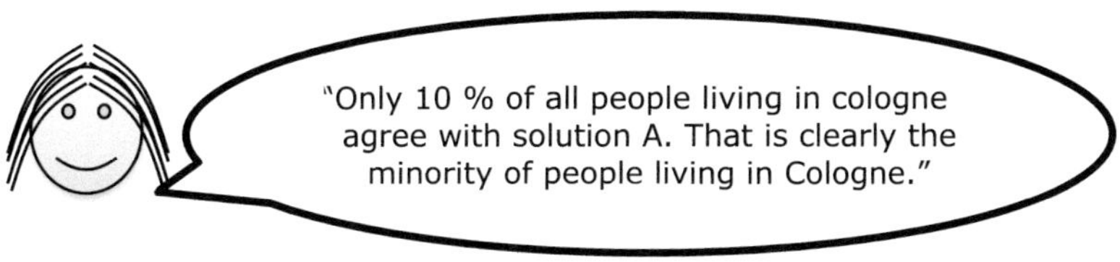

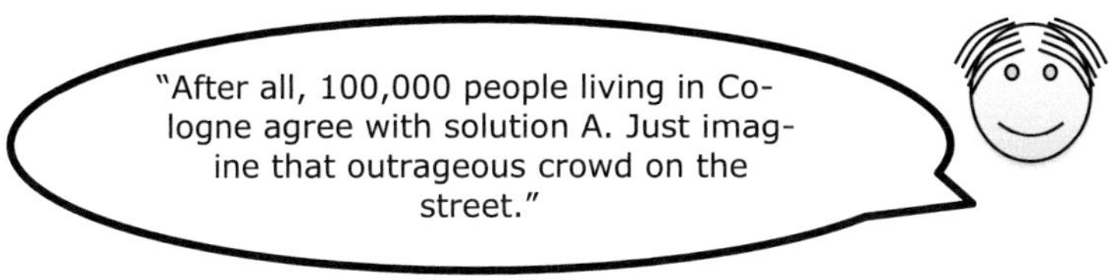

Another example:

The following data resulted in a (fictional) survey about the subject. "How did you like the first-run movie?"

good	65 %
bad	35 %

Obviously, the majority of the people questioned did like the movie.

Result: notably more good than bad.

Let us see if the results possibly change if we give three alternatives instead of two (good vs. bad) three:

outstanding	30 %
good	35 %
bad	35 %

Result: the same amount of people that said good, also said bad.

Or if we even give six different possibilities to answer:

outstanding	30 %
good	20 %
rather good	15 %
rather bad	5 %
bad	25 %
very bad	5 %

Result: more bad than good.

That means: depending on how we collect the data (only two possibilities to answer or six possibilities) it may end up in clearly different (or even opposite) results.

Depending on the direction, you want to manipulate the data you can change the options. Obviously, data can be manipulated so far that you can actually get the opposite statement of what originally was correct.

Just for clarification: the reader should not be encouraged to manipulate but he should be able to recognize when and how manipulation is tried to influence him and that he knows how to react to it.

Are 2 times 2 equal 2 to the power of 2?

In year X, the average European eats 100 pork cutlets. In year Y, he eats twice as much, i.e., 200 pork cutlets. Therefore, we have the following pictographic display:

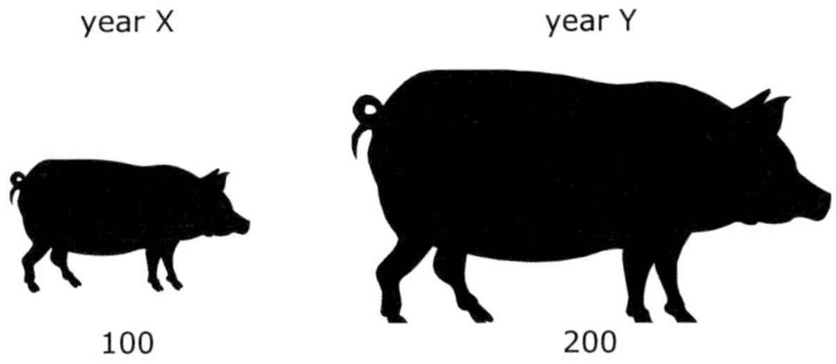

Is it right? No – it is wrong! And why? Because the second pig is not displayed in the right proportion to the first one.

The pig on the right side is not displayed twice as big as the one on the left side. It is more likely four times as big. Because it is doubled in length and height. Therefore, 2 times 2 are not 2 to the power of 2.

For clarification, let us demonstrate it with squares.

To double, looks like this:

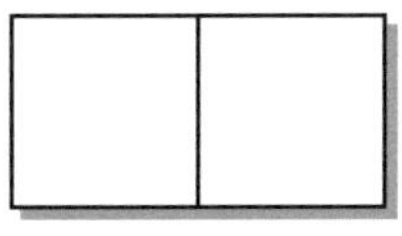

Or so:

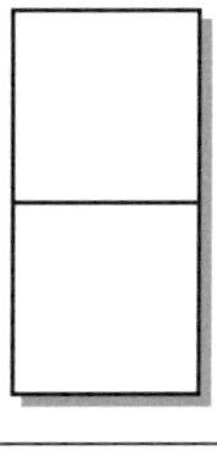

But not like that:

This pictographic display of our pig is more likely correct:

In reality, numbers are rarely exactly 100 or 200. They are most likely 97 or 213 so that possible manipulation is even more difficult to recognize.

In a three dimensional sample the third dimension is added. Therefore, the size does not increase four times. It expands exponentially at the same time, namely 8 times.

"It goes radically uphill"

"You can clearly see it in this graphic chart, which I have prepared especially for you, dear ladies and gentlemen. Please look here. Impressive? Isn't it?"

These are the word of a speaker while he is pointing at the graphic chart. An admiring murmur goes throughout the audience.

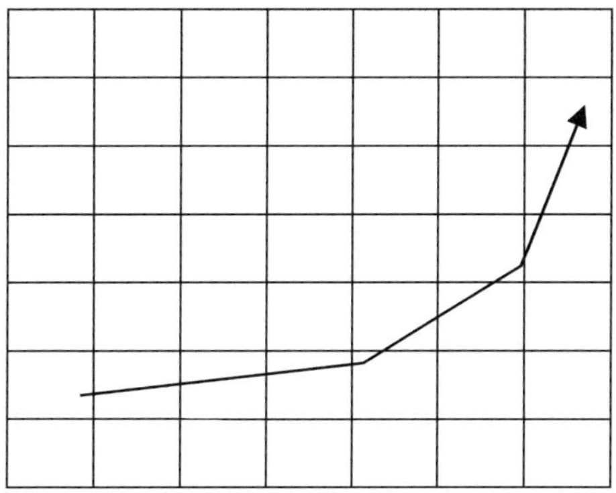

Indeed, somehow the graphic chart does look impressive.

However, there is no coordinates on the legend. If you pull down the y-axis then the picture looks like that.

Or like that:

Not that impressive anymore, right? If we stretch the distances on the x-axis a little bit more we will get the following picture:

The arrowhead clearly signals 'it keeps on going uphill'.

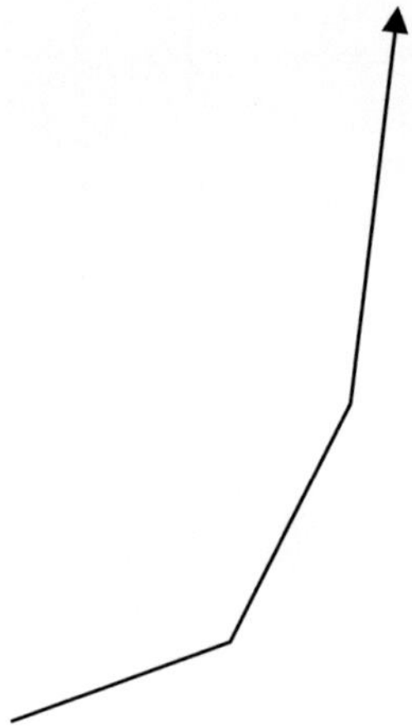

This graphic chart only pleases us if it demonstrates how little the cost grew in the last three years …

For stockholders we use the original graphic chart with the x-axis tightened together a little bit.

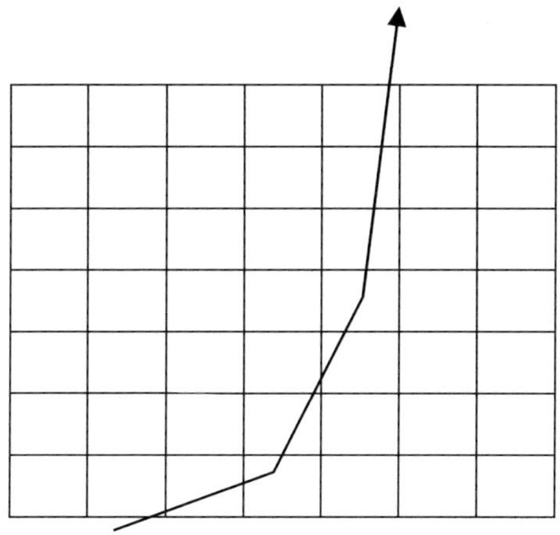

Convinced?

Pie Chart

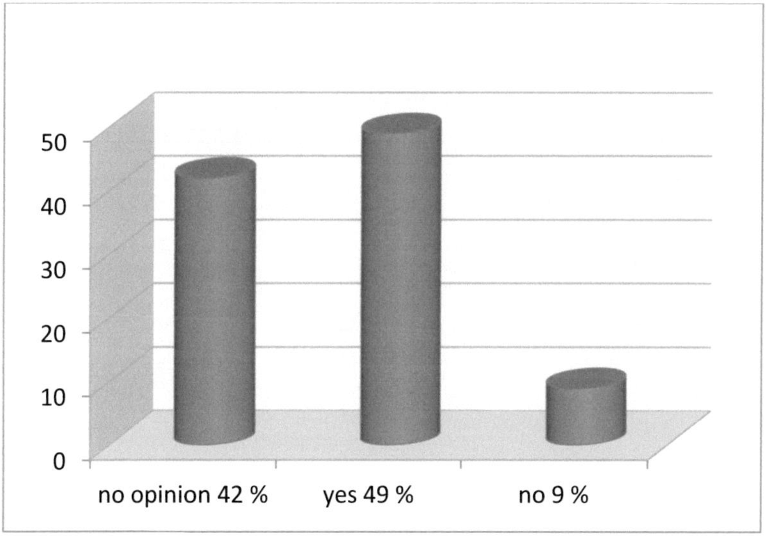

How do you read the displayed pie chart above?

- The majority of the interviewees agreed (49 %)
- The majority of the interviewees did not agree or they had no opinion (51 %)
- Only 9 % of the interviewees voted 'no'

Does that example seem to be too extreme? Can you imagine that you can get to a completely different view just by reading the two statements starting with "The majority …" if you do not have any other details?

And do not forget: both statements are true even if they somehow express the opposite.

All are the best

German state	area in 1000 km^2	inhabitants in thousands	capital	inhabitants in thousands	inhabitants per km^2
Baden-Wuerttemberg	35.8	10,476	Stuttgart	582	293
Bavaria	70.5	12,155	Munich	1,195	172
Berlin	0.9	3,387	Berlin	3,387	3,799
Bremen	0.4	663	Bremen	540	1,640
Mecklenburg-Western Pomerania	23.2	1,789	Schwerin	1,784	77
North Rhine-Westphalia	34.1	18,000	Düsseldorf	569	528
Saxony	18.4	4,460	Dresden	477	242

- North Rhine-Westphalia is the state with the highest amount of inhabitants.
- Bavaria is the state with the highest / smallest ... in Germany.
- Berlin is the state whose capital has the highest number of inhabitants among all capitals in Germany.
- Saarland is the state with the highest / smallest ... in Germany.
- Mecklenburg-Western Pomerania is the state with lowest amount of inhabitants per km².

(All information refer to Germany; data from Federal Statistic Office, Germany, 1999)

By the way:

- 90 % of all patients stay alive (sounds better than)
- 10 % of all patients die
- or: 10 % of all patients inside a hospital die (therefore: do not go to a hospital)

Again, by the way:

- That was so far the worst storm
- the hottest February 1st since 53 years (what about February 2nd?)

The best space-related stories

At the end of January, the television station VOX showed that competing television stations did separate surveys to figure out who has the best space-related stories.

The result was always in favor of the commissioning company: the Forsa Institute sees the Kirch-group with Sat.1 and ProSieben in front and the Enigma Institute is in favor of RTLII (Source: Der Spiegel 4/2002, pg. 103).

German women enjoy and remain silent

By the way: German women enjoy and remain silent. That is how it was written in a newspaper: due to a representative survey of the Forsa Institute about 1,000 women between the age 20 to 60 years for the German magazine 'marie Claire' indicates that every German woman has 4.4 lovers in her life.

Just four years before, there was a similar survey and the result was that women had 3.4 lovers in a lifetime and that 47 % [1)] of all women had (at least) one lover. After all 3 % of the interviewed women said that, they had 11 or more lovers.

Unbelievable but even 7 % of the interviewed women said that they even had once 2 lovers [2)] <u>at the same time</u>. Every 10th women had sex with a married man according to the survey but they did not mean their husband. All in all, 8 % remembered that they betrayed their husband before.

Remarks of the author:

[1)] It is not clear if the remaining 57 % of women never had a lover. Or should it mean that they just had one lover in their entire life?

[2)] Statistics does not say if it means an 'orgy' or if the women had two lovers over a certain period of time. The words '<u>at the same time</u>' are not distinct.

Chapter 9 – Organisation

Conference room

"A conference is a meeting,
where lots of people go,
but there is little outcome."
Werner Paul Walther Finck, German cabaret artist
(1902 - 1978)

The appropriate room for a discussion

Are you planning a conversation/discussion? It could be situated in your (own) office, in the cafeteria, in a conference room, or in a guest room.

It also could be a television studio or many other places. However, not every room is appropriate for a conversation/discussion.

It is important to consider whether the audience is participating and what the size of the potential audience might be. The following attributes influence the success of a conversation round:

- Location of the room?
- Own office?
- Conference room?
- Television studio?
- Size of the room in m^2
- Is there a microphone system available and how does it work? Who is handling the system?
- Is there an echo, distortion or feedback?
- How many chairs does the room hold?
- Are the participants sitting in a circle?
- Should the participants sit behind tables?
- Where should the moderator be?
- With more furniture, more sound will be absorbed.
- How and where should the audience be placed?
- Is there daylight and are there any windows in the room?

- How can the room be dimed if slides are to be presented?
- Is it possible to open windows for better air circulation and/or does the room have air conditioning? How can it be adjusted?
- How can the room's lighting be adjusted? Is there a dimmer?
- Is it necessary to have IT equipment or media?
- Where can the moderator place his or her notes?
- Are there enough electrical outlets for all of the equipment needed?
- When can the moderator access the room to set things up? Is there a key to the room? And who will provide it?

Note cards

Do you need to use note cards? Remember: A note card is not meant to hold the complete text.

A detailed manuscript does not belong on a note card! If you want to read your speech from a manuscript, it will then become a <u>reading</u>, and not a <u>presentation</u>.

A note card can be used to jog your memory in all types of presentations, however.

A good note card should have the following characteristics:

- cardboard, not paper
- A6 or C7 size
- unfolded
- not in pure white
- colors that make a positive impact (white, blue, green, grey), but not neon if possible
- number the note cards if you use several
- make sure your writing is large and clear
- write only on one side
- <u>do not</u> write full sentences, <u>do</u> use keywords
  - dates
  - names
  - quotes
  - reminders, for example, when a slide should be shown
  - statistics
  - if necessary, your first sentence

Work with symbols, for example:

- don't forget to smile (smiley ☺)
- make eye contact (eye 👁)
- speak slowly (running figure 🏃)
- insert quote (speech balloon 💬)
- insert statistic (graph symbol, arrow pointing upward ↗)
- don't use any non-words (lightning bolt ϟ)

Just let your imagination run wild!

A note card can also serve to calm you:

- it can give you a sense of security
- it can quiet your nerves
- you have something to 'hold onto'

However: it can also form a mini-barrier between you and your listeners.

Hand-outs and documents

When you need supporting documents for a discussion, they should be prepared in advance.

Possible procedures might include the following.

- Brainstorming – to accumulate material
  - to gather ideas
  - without choosing a specific order of preference
  - no killer phrases; no evaluation
- Evaluate – select
  - evaluate the feasibility of ideas
  - drop the non-feasible ideas
  - stick to the feasible ideas
- Sort – select – settle
  - sort feasible ideas again
  - determine a definite selection
  - drop the non-feasible ideas
- prepare an outline – put in order
  - draw a specific order of precedence (decide the correct order; what builds up on something else?)
- attach graphic material
  - graphics, drawings, attach pictures to the manuscript
  - prepare slides
- Layout
  - insert and integrate graphical material into the layout
  - maybe complete animation in Power-Point

"Where are the restrooms?"

At the very beginning of a seminar, it is important to clear up all the organizational aspects with your listeners. This includes:

- Information on the length of the program and/or end of the event
- Information on the number, kind and length of breaks
- Information on where to find the restrooms
    - "You can wash your hands ..."
- Information on how to regulate the room temperature (windows, air conditioning/heating)
- Information on smoking during the event or breaks
- Information on any materials to be handed out or available study aids
- Information on how participants can ask questions or make comments (calling out, raising a hand, etc.)
- Reminder to switch off mobile phones
- Perhaps some remarks on the structure of your presentation
- Perhaps a remark that all examples apply equally to men and women, even if for simplicity's sake the male form is used.

In the case of short talks or presentations, the points listed here are of course less important. If you are working for a client, then give some thought to the following:

- Who am I addressing?
- Who can I turn to if I have questions during my work?
- Will I be introduced to my audience?
- Which organizational points should I mention on behalf of my client?
- Does a list of attendees have to be made?
- Will the listeners receive a certificate of participation?
- Will the listeners be given a feedback sheet to fill out?

Structure of the Presentation

By parts of a presentation, we mean: introduction, main body and conclusion. However, as you will see, there are other parts as well.

Some presentations are more or less like a sales pitch. And almost every conversation represents a sales pitch. Let us compare the phases of a typical sales pitch with the phases of a presentation:

As you can see, a presentation is structured almost exactly like a sales pitch.

On point 3

- Arouse interest:

  "The topic is important to you because ..."
- Name a goal:

  "Today, I will show you ..."
- Find out what listeners already know:

  "Have you heard of ...?"
- Create a relationship with actual practice:

  "In your area of work, this is ..."

On point 4

- Get your listeners involved:

  "What would you do if ...?"
- Provide some tangible illustrations:

  "Compare it with the following situation ..."
- Confirm interim results attained:

  "We have already established the following ..."
- Clear up any uncertainties – make sure your listeners understand: "Are there any points that are still unclear? Do you have any questions?"

Index

Editor and translator

Thomas Schommers holds an A.L.M. in Sustainability and Environmental Management from Harvard University and a B.A. (honours) in Asian Pacific Business Administration from the University of Hertfordshire, UK.

He also is a certified Business Mediator by the Chamber of Commerce and Industry in Munich and a certified China-Manager by the Chamber of Commerce and Industry in Hannover, Germany.

Currently, he works for ISR – International School on the Rhine gGmbH, Germany in the field of public affairs, public relations and marketing.

He is a member of the Curriculum Advisory Board of the Maastricht School of Management, NL. Since 2007, he has been the team-building coach of their Executive MBA program (in cooperation with Cologne Business School, Germany) and MBA program.

He is an associate lecturer at University of Applied Sciences Bremen for "Doing Business in China." He is the President of the German-American Association Neuss.

He was the head of "Studium Generale" at European University of Applied Sciences (EUFH). At EUFH, he was also an associate lecturer for management/negotiation techniques with Asian people, focusing on the Chinese 36 Stratagems and Sun Tzu, project and change management.

In 2005, he began working for Horst-Hanisch-Seminare Bonn, Germany as freelance coach on Asian issues and on coaching, etiquette, team building, and corporate identity.

He has translated from German to English and edited the book "Discussion – Mastering the Skills of Moderation" by Horst Hanisch. Additionally, he has worked as a freelance consultant, researcher, and management coach.

He has completed projects for the European University of Applied Sciences, Germany, Cologne Business School, Germany; Henley Management College, UK; Maastricht School of Management, Netherlands; Sophia University, Tokyo, Japan; bci - best connection international, Germany, Business Management Services (U.S. agent of KKU), U.S.A.; The Lausanne Consulting Group, UK; United Parcel Service, Germany, the U.S. Consulate General in Düsseldorf, Germany and the U.S. Embassy in Berlin, Germany.

12 Ratgeber in der kleinen Knigge-Reihe

Der kleine ... -Knigge [2100]

Anstands- und Banausen-...
Business- und Kunden-...
Büro- und Kollegen-...
Gäste- und Gastgeber-...
Gesellschafts- und Freunde-...
Outfit- und Stil-...
Interkulturelle- und Auslands-...
Bewerbungs- und Vorstellungs-...
Event- und Feste-...
Gastro- und Tischsitten-...
Speisen- und Exoten-...
Trinkkultur- und Getränke-...

Je 88 Seiten

Das kleine Handbuch der Rhetorik [2100]

Erfolgreich reden „Die Kunst, flott vorzutragen"
Körpersprache einsetzen „Mit Händen und Füßen sprechen"
Gezielt trainieren „Ich will endlich erfolgreich präsentieren!"
Nervosität austricksen „Mir zittern die Knie"
Begeistert überzeugen „Das rhetorische Feuer entfachen"
Unterschwellig manipulieren „Ich kriege dich schon!"
Wahrnehmung verzerren „Ich glaub' nur, was ich sehe."
Einwände entkräften „Das ist doch gar nicht machbar! – Oder doch?"
Gespräche führen „Zielorientierte und zeitsparende Gesprächslenkung"
Meetings leiten „Besprechungen erfolgreich führen"
Geschicktes Nudging „Das versteckte Anschubsen"
Interviews führen „Darf ich Sie mal fragen?"
Je 100 Seiten

Das Märchen der ...

professionellen Argumentation
harmlosen Fragen
sauberen Wahrheit
vertrauenswürdigen Fairness

... in der Rhetorik [2100]
Je 100 Seiten

4 Ratgeber in der Ego-Management-Reihe

Persönlichkeits-Management – Ego-Knigge 2100 Soft Skills, Selbst-Reflexion und Selbst-Bewusstsein

Stress-Management – Ego-Knigge 2100 Lampenfieber, Stressoren, Gerüchte, Mobbing, Burnout, Stressvermeidung

Zeit-Management – Ego-Knigge 2100 Umgang mit der Zeit, Organisation von Arbeitsabläufen, Perfektionismus, Zielsetzung

Gedächtnis-Management – Ego-Knigge 2100 Gehirn, Intelligenz, Schwachsinn – Hochbegabung, Gedächtnis, Lerntechniken.

Jeder Ratgeber 104 Seiten, A5, kartoniert

4 Ratgeber der Reihe Lebenseinstellung

Aberglauben-Knigge 2100 Von schwarzen Katzen, der linken Hand des Teufels und den Glücksbringern
Lügen- und Egoismus-Knigge 2100 Überleben durch Flunkern, Schummeln und Täuschen! Macht, Respekt, Wertschätzung? Lebenslüge und Lebensschutz
Glücks-Knigge 2100 Vom Glücklichsein, positiven Denken und von Freundschaften
Angst- und Optimismus-Knigge 2100 Die Furcht beherrschen, Ängste nutzen und positiv durchs Leben gehen.

Jeder Ratgeber 216 Seiten, A5, kartoniert

3 Ratgeber Bräutigam, Braut und Brautpaar

Bräutigam-Knigge 2100 Verlobung und Polterabend, Schwiegereltern und das Ja-Wort, Hochzeits-Outfit und Hochzeits-Kutsche

Braut-Knigge 2100 Brautkleid und Accessoires, Das große Hochzeitsfest, Höhepunkte und Hochzeitstanz

Brautpaar-Knigge 2100 Historisches und Sonderbares, Planung und Organisation, Aberglaube und Hochzeitsbräuche.

Jeder Ratgeber 104 Seiten, A5, kartoniert

3 Ratgeber Selbst-Coaching

Selbstbewusstsein Knigge 2100 Ich bin, ich kann, ich will. Das eigene Leben bestimmen, Soft Skills, The Winner 1.

Selbstwertgefühl Knigge 2100 Steh auf! Werde aktiv! Zeige Profil! Das eigene Leben beeinflussen, Motivation, The Winner 2.

Selbstoptimierung Knigge 2100 Optimistischer, attraktiver, authentischer. Das eigene Leben gestalten, Ansprüche, The Winner 3.

Jeder Ratgeber 120 Seiten, A5, kartoniert

Leben und Lifestyle

Adam allein auf der Welt Knigge 2100 Ein Buch mit Bildern vom ersten Menschen, seinen Gedanken und seiner Körpersprache, 104 Seiten, A5, ca. 155 Fotos

Jugend-Knigge 2100 Knigge für junge Leute und Berufseinsteiger, 152 Seiten

Alters-Knigge 2100 Abgehängt und abgeschoben? Altersdiskriminierung? Akzeptanz des Älterwerdens!, 152 Seiten

Zukunfts-Knigge 2100 Verfall der Sitten und Verlust der Wertschätzung? Umgangsformen in 100 Jahren. Zusammenleben mit Menschen, Maschinen und menschenähnlichen Robotern, 172 Seiten A5 kartoniert

KI-Knigge 2100 Leben mit der Künstlichen Intelligenz! Veränderungen im realen Umgang?, 196 Seiten A5 kartoniert

Wertschätzung-Knigge 2100 Gleichberechtigung, Gender und Respekt, Sexuelle Orientierung, Umgang bei Diskriminierung und Mobbing, 152 Seiten A5

Hochzeits-Knigge 2100 Hochzeitsbräuche, Geschenke, Brautjungfer, Trauung, Festgäste und Festmahl, 310 Seiten A5

Ü65- und Senioren-Knigge 2100 Die junge Alten und die alten Jungen, Kommunikation und Verständnis zwischen den Generationen, 180 Seiten A5

Blumen-Knigge 2100 Historisches, Mystisches, Festliches, Blumensprache, Umgang mit Blumen-Präsenten, 144 Seiten A5

Bekleidung! Ausdruck der Persönlichkeit – Lukas‘ Outfit-Knigge 2100, 196 Seiten A5

Nudel-Knigge 2100 Himmlische Teigwaren, 140 Seiten A5

Der Interkulturelle Kompetenz-Knigge 2100 Kultur, Kompetenz, Eindrücke – Gesten, Rituale, Zeitempfinden – Berichte, Tipps, Erlebnisse, 240 Seiten A5

China-Deutschland-Knigge 2100 Chinesen in Deutschland, 104 Seiten A5

Dschungel-Knigge 2100 Umgang in ungewohnter Umgebung, 192 Seiten A5

Von allen guten Geistern verlassen-Knigge 2100, 132 Seiten A5

Der Dicke-Knigge 2100 Aus dem prallen Leben des Dicken, 104 Seiten A5

Typisch Frau – Typisch Mann Knigge 2100 Unterschiede und Gemeinsamkeiten im Umgang mit dem anderen Geschlecht, 128 Seiten A5

Kulinarischer und Gastronomischer Knigge 2100 284 Seiten A5

Klo- und Pinkel-Knigge 2100 Vom privaten und öffentlichen Bedürfnis - Umgangsformen im Tabu-Bereich, 104 Seiten A5

Alles hat seine Zeit-Knigge 2100 Umgang mit der Zeit, 294 Seite A5

Omi hüpf‘ mal Märchen meiner Großmutter, Erlebnisse ihre Jugend und wahre Geschichten meines Vaters von und über Omi Rickchen, Hardcover, 312 Seiten

Der Hunde-Knigge 2100 Umgang mit dem Hund – Hundesprache – Der Hund in der Gesellschaft, 180 Seiten A5

Welcome to Germany-Knigge 2100 Umgangsformen, Verhaltensmuster und gesellschaftliches Miteinander im deutschsprachigen Europa, 108 Seiten A5

Besuch willkommen Knigge 2100 Einladung, Gast, Geschenk, Empfang, Feier, Gastfreundschaft, 200 Seiten A5

Leben, Tod und Ansichten Austausch mit Berühmtheiten über Wichtiges und Unwichtiges im Leben, 116 Seiten A5

Last List Leid 2100 Verlogene Welt?, 160 Seiten A5

Mensch Macht Mörder 2100 Verfall der Umgangsformen?, 260 Seiten A5

Tod, Trauer, Totenkult-Knigge 2100 Sterben, Trost, Takt, Bestatten, Tradition, Vorsorge, Tabus, Vergänglichkeit und Sonderbares, 212 Seiten A5

Corona Knigge 2100 Umgang mit dem Virus, 88 Seiten 12x19, kartoniert

Das kleine Knigge-Quiz 2100 96 Seiten, 12x19 cm, kartoniert

Leben und Lifestyle

Rhetorik, Soft Skills, Hochschule, Beruf

Rhetorik ist Silber Von den ersten Schritten zu einer perfekten Präsentation, 336 Seiten A5, kartoniert, Zeichnungen

Moderation ist Gold Gesprächsführung, Umfragen, Talkrunden und Manipulation, 274 Seiten A5, kartoniert, Zeichnungen

Lebhafte Körpersprache in Vorträgen, Präsentationen, Gesprächen, 218 Seiten A5, kartoniert, ca. 290 Zeichnungen

Rhetoric – Mastering the Art of Persuasion, 222 Seiten A5, kartoniert

Discussion – Mastering the Skills of Moderation, 192 Seiten A5, kartoniert

Body Language in Europe, 196 Seiten A5, kartoniert, ca. 290 Zeichnungen

Das große Buch der Kommunikation und der Gesprächsführung ^{2100}, 460 Seiten A5, kartoniert, Zeichnungen

Das große Buch der Rhetorik ^{2100} Tacheles reden; Präsentieren; manipulieren und überzeugen, 452 Seiten A5, kartoniert, viele Darstellungen

Trickreiche Rhetorik ^{2100} Psychologische Gesprächsführung, manipulierende Darstellung, unaufdringliches Nudging, 448 Seiten A5, kartoniert, Zeichnungen

Körpersprache ^{2100} **– Lüge, Verrat, Macht**, Im Beruf, vor Gericht, beim Flirt – Gewinnerpose und Demutshaltung; 440 Seiten A5, kartoniert, über 400 Zeichnungen

Soft Skills-Knigge ^{2100} Soziale, Persönlichkeit, Selbstmanagement, 480 Seiten A5, kartoniert, viele Darstellungen

Schlagfertigkeit-, Spontaneität-, Stegreif-Knigge ^{2100} Impulsiv handeln, verbale Angriffe kontern, Störungen entwaffnen, 104 Seiten A5

Pitch Skills und Überzeugungs-Knigge ^{2100} Elevator Pitch, Geldgeber beeindrucken, Feuer versprühen, 128 Seiten A5, kartoniert

Smalltalk-Knigge ^{2100} Vom kleinen Gespräch bis zum charmanten Flirt - Kontakt ausbauen, Sympathie zeigen, Begehrlichkeit wecken, 100 Seiten A5

Quassel-Knigge ^{2100} Quasseln, Quatschen, Quengeln oder Lebenswichtige Kommunikation – Gezielt eingesetzte Rhetorik – Aussagekräftiges Profil zeigen, 112 Seiten A5

Die moderne Führungskraft ^{2100} **Online und Präsenz,** Handbuch für souveräne Vorgesetzte und solche, die es werden wollen, 252 Seiten A5, kartoniert, Zeichnungen

Emotionale Rhetorik im Leben und rund um den Tod ^{2100} Vielfältige Kommunikation – Fiktiver Interview-Austausch mit Berühmtheiten, 260 Seiten A5

Innere Rhetorik ^{2100} Zielführende Kommunikation mit sich selbst, 140 Seiten A5

Kriegerische Rhetorik ^{2100} Sensible Diplomatie, einfühlsame Empathie, 156 Seiten A5

Blumige Rhetorik ^{2100} Zielführende Kommunikation mit sich selbst, 140 Seiten A5

Alles hat seine Zeit – Knigge ^{2100} Umgang mit der Zeit, 294 Seiten A5

Hochschul-Knigge ^{2100} Studentischer Umgang, 132 Seiten A5, kartoniert, Fotos

Jugend-Karriere-Knigge ^{2100} 224 Seiten A5, kartoniert, Zeichnungen, Checklisten

Bewerbungs-Knigge ^{2100} **für Frauen – Tina bewirbt sich / Bewerbungs-Knigge** ^{2100} **für Männer – Tom bewirbt sich**, Vorbereitung, Wahl der Kleidung, Verhalten beim Bewerbungsgespräch, je 128 Seiten A5, kartoniert, Fotos, Checklisten

Online-Bewerbungsgespräche-Knigge ^{2100} **Vorstellungsgespräche auf Distanz – Tina und Tom bewerben sich digital**, 128 Seiten A5, kartoniert, Zeichnungen

Kreativitäts-Knigge ^{2100}, Visionärhaft denken, Scheuklappen sprengen, Mentales Risiko eingehen, 164 Seiten A5, kartoniert

Team und Typ-Knigge ^{2100}, Ich und Wir, Typen und Charaktere, Team-Entwicklung, 128 Seiten A5, kartoniert, viele Darstellungen

Die flotte Generation Y im 21. Jahrhundert, selbstbewusst – lebensbetonend – flexibel, 116 Seiten A5, kartoniert, Zeichnungen

Die flotte Generation Z im 21. Jahrhundert, entscheidungsfreudig – effizient – eigenverantwortlich, 140 Seiten A5, kartoniert, Zeichnungen

Tele-Meeting ^{2100}, Digitale Konferenz, Online-Unterricht, Homeoffice, 104 Seiten A5, kartoniert

Rhetorik, Soft Skills, Hochschule, Beruf

Englisch: